The Drum Lesson Manual

Your Complete Guide to Better Drumming

By Scott Strunk

Copyright 2012 Scott Strunk Music. All rights reserved.
No part of this book may be reproduced in part or whole without the express written permission of Scott Strunk Music.
ISBN-13: 9780615569864
ISBN-10: 0615569862

Introduction

The ideas in this book—written for beginners, professional drummers, and everyone in between—come from my 30 plus years of studying, playing, and teaching drums. As a student, I did not find one book that covered all of the information I needed to become a proficient drummer; as a veteran teacher of approximately 40 students a week for over 20 years, I wanted to share the methods I have refined in my successful teaching practice.

If you are a beginner, this book will help you get started with grip and reading. I present practical applications to show why you are practicing these basic skills and give you advice on how to practice. If you are a professional, the challenging exercises included in here will keep your skills tuned up. I encourage you to build upon the ideas in this book to inspire your playing.

Part 1 focuses on grip, technique, and basic reading of rhythms. Part 2 focuses on reading rhythms at all levels proficiently. Part 3 focuses on the 40 standard snare drum rudiments, sticking, and technique exercises. Part 4 focuses on drum set techniques, coordination, grooves, and soloing in different genres of music.

Although this book progresses in a logical sequence, I recommend skipping around to work on specific skills. If you can complete this book correctly, you will have a solid foundation and play better at every level. I have also incorporated some of the ideas from great drum books that I've used throughout my years in drumming, which I have named and recommended at the end of this book.

Enjoy your process towards better drumming!

Thank You

First I would like to thank ALL of my current and former students. You have helped me to write this book! It is because of each of you that this book exists.

Thanks to Bobby Grauso and all my great teachers throughout the years.

My lovely wife, Maria, thanks for using my book at your school and for helping to shape it.

Thanks Pam Hubbard and Julian Kim for editing and proofreading.

Thanks Mary Anne Lynch at mpowerdesign.com for all of your time.

Thanks Dave Anthony and Dave Owens for your feedback and support.

Thanks Dr. Mark Jeffery, Steve Young, and Steve Orkin for your help.

Thanks Dan Komoda for the pictures and Chris Marcus for the cover.

Contents

Part 1: Introduction to Basics: Grip, Techniques, Reading, and Rudiments

Matched Grip 2
Traditional Grip 5
Music Notation 1: Introducing Quarter Notes 7
Time Signature 7
Half / Tap Stroke 8
Full / Rebound Stroke 9
Music Notation 2: Introducing 8th Notes 10
Introducing Rudiments 11
Single Stroke Roll 11
Double Stroke Roll 12
Multiple Bounce Stroke Roll 13
Paradiddles. 14
Flams 15
Drags 16
Music Notation 3: Introducing 16th Notes 17
Basic Technique and Rudiment Exercises 18

Part 2: Reading Rhythms

Reading Rhythm Exercises: Whole Notes, Half Notes, Quarter Notes, 8th Notes,
16th Notes, and Rests 22
4 Bar Note and Rest Combinations: Whole Notes through 8th Notes 23
4 Bar Note and Rest Combinations: 8th through 16th Notes 24
8th and 16th Notes Connected 26
Dotted Notes and Ties 28
Subdivisions with Triplets 29
Quarter and 8th Note Triplet Exercises 30
Syncopation 1 31
Rolls in Rhythm 32
16th Note Triplet Exercises 34
Syncopation 2 35
Cut Time 36
6/8 Time Signature 37
Subdivisions Adding 5s, 7s, and 32nd Notes 38
Exercises in Various Time Signatures 39

Contents

Part 3: The 40 Standard Snare Drum Rudiments and Technique Exercises

The 40 Standard Snare Drum Rudiments 42
Sticking Exercises 47
Accent Exercises 49
Rudiment Combos and Technique Exercises 51

Part 4: Drum Set Technique, Coordination Exercises, Styles, Grooves, and Soloing

Bass Drum and Hi-Hat Pedal Technique 54
Basic Drum Set Coordination 55
Basic Drum Set Coordination and Fills 56
Drum Set Coordination Exercises 57
Linear Grooves 64
Fill and Solo Ideas 66
Jazz Time 69
Jazz Time and Coordination Exercises 70
32 Bar Tune "AABA" Form / Cross Stick Technique 73
Jazz Beats 74
Jazz Band Audition Pages: Jazz, Latin, Rock, World Beats, and Brushes 75
Latin Grooves and Coordination 78
Grooves in Various Time Signatures 79
Playing Time with Melodic Ideas 80
Soloing with Melodic Ideas 81
Picking Up Hits 82

Appendix

How to Practice 86
Music Terminology 88
Recommended Books 89

Part 1: Introduction to Basics: Grip, Techniques, Reading, and Rudiments

Matched Grip

Matched grip is when your right and left hand grip "match" each other.

1. Hold your sticks at the balance point. Divide the sticks into 3 equal parts. Place your thumb flat at the rear third of the stick.

2. With your thumbs flat at the rear third, gently place your 1st and 2nd fingers on the sticks. The 1st finger should touch the sticks at the top knuckle and lie naturally, slightly in front of the thumb toward the tip of the stick. This creates a three-finger **fulcrum**/pivot point for the stick.

3. Your thumbs should be flat on the sticks. The sticks should look like a straight extension of your thumbs. Your thumbs should not touch your 1st finger under the sticks—there should be space. If you turn your hands to look at your palm you should see space on the sticks between your 1st fingers and thumbs.

4. Gently place fingers 4 and 5 on sticks. These fingers, especially your pinkies, will remain touching the sticks.

5. The butt of the stick should be lined up in your palm with the outside wrist bone on your pinky side.

6. Turn your palms to face the floor. The sticks should now make a **90° angle** pointing to the center of the drum. When looking down at your hands you should see all of your knuckles.

7. Your elbows should be completely relaxed at your sides. Don't hold your elbows up, or hold them tightly to your side.

* VERY IMPORTANT: Steps 1–7 are the start position. You will build everything upon this foundation.
* Remember the word "match"—your hands, arms, and wrists should "match" each other always. Constantly check yourself, especially at the beginning. Always be aware of what you are doing and how you are doing it.

8. Place yourself in the "Start Position." While doing all the above, hold your sticks off the drum 3–5 inches with your fingers gently on the sticks.

Exercise: Easy Reset
This usually takes care of steps 1–8 above naturally.

Hold your sticks at the balance point in the fulcrum. Drop your arms to your side. Bring your sticks up to the *start position* with the sticks pointing to the center of the drum; your palms face the floor, your sticks are at a 90° angle and 3–5 inches off the drum.

Exercise: Practice Fulcrum in the Air
Using the grip above, hold your sticks one at a time in front of your face with your palm facing your nose and practice this:

1. Let the stick fall away from your nose, open your fingers and pivot on your FULCRUM, NOT YOUR WRIST! Your wrist should stay straight and not break or bend backwards. Your fingers should touch the sticks at all times.
2. Pull the stick back to your palm slowly and controlled using your fingers.
3. Repeat #1 and #2. Keep practicing this until you are comfortable. This is what should happen when you are playing as the sticks are rebounding.

Pictures of Matched Grip

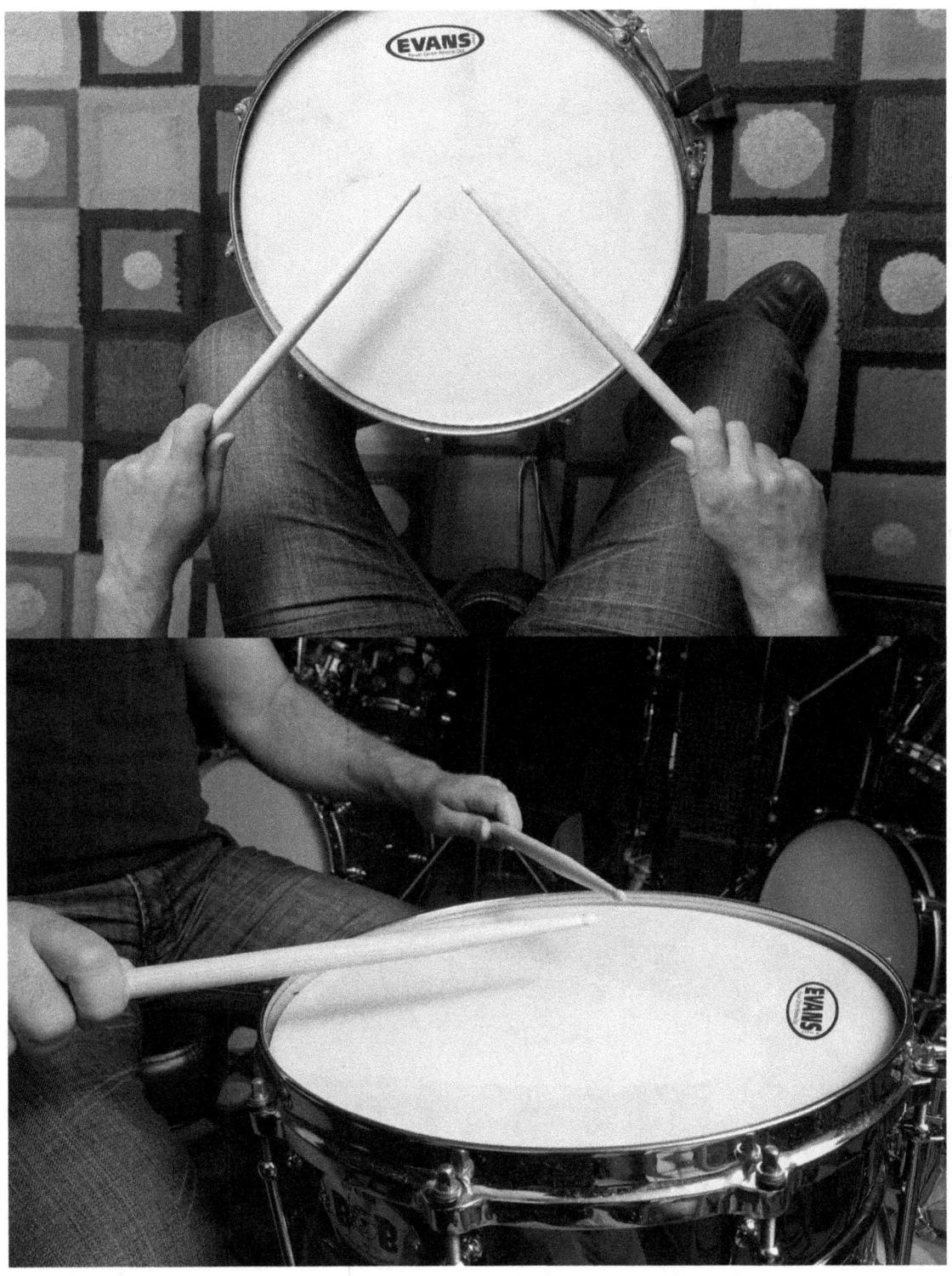

Pictures of Matched Grip

Traditional Grip

Traditional grip is a way of holding the left stick. This grip was originally used when marching with a drum hung over one shoulder on a sling. This would tilt the drum at an angle that would cause the left hand to be raised in an awkward position unless the stick was held differently.

1. Your right hand is held the same as matched grip.

2. Drop your left hand to your side and let it hang naturally. With your left elbow relaxed, raise your hand as if you are about to shake hands.

3. Place the stick in the base of your thumb at the balance point of the stick. The stick should now be in the web of your thumb.

4. The stick should intersect the web of your thumb at the rear third of the stick. This is the fulcrum/pivot point for the stick.

5. Place your 1st finger on top of stick. Your 1st finger should rest on top of the stick at the bottom of the nail. Your 1st finger should have a natural curve as it rests on the stick.

6. Place your 2nd finger slightly on top of the stick. Your 2nd finger should rest on the stick at the bottom of the finger, just under the nail.

7. Your 4th and 5th finger should be underneath the stick.

* Your sticks should make the same 90° angle, pointing to the center of the drum, as matched grip.

Exercise 1: Fulcrum Only
Practice bouncing and rebounding the stick in the fulcrum using your thumb only (see #4 above). Do this without adding fingers 1–5.

Exercise 2: Add Fingers
Now practice bouncing and rebounding adding all other fingers. THE BOUNCE AND REBOUND SHOULD NOT CHANGE WHEN YOU ADD YOUR OTHER FINGERS TO THE FULCRUM.

Exercise 3: 8 Off 8 On
Practice switching back and forth between the fulcrum only grip and the complete grip, and work on not letting the stroke change. Practice 8 fulcrum rebounds just using thumbs, then 8 more adding fingers. There should be no rebound difference.

Pictures of Traditional Grip

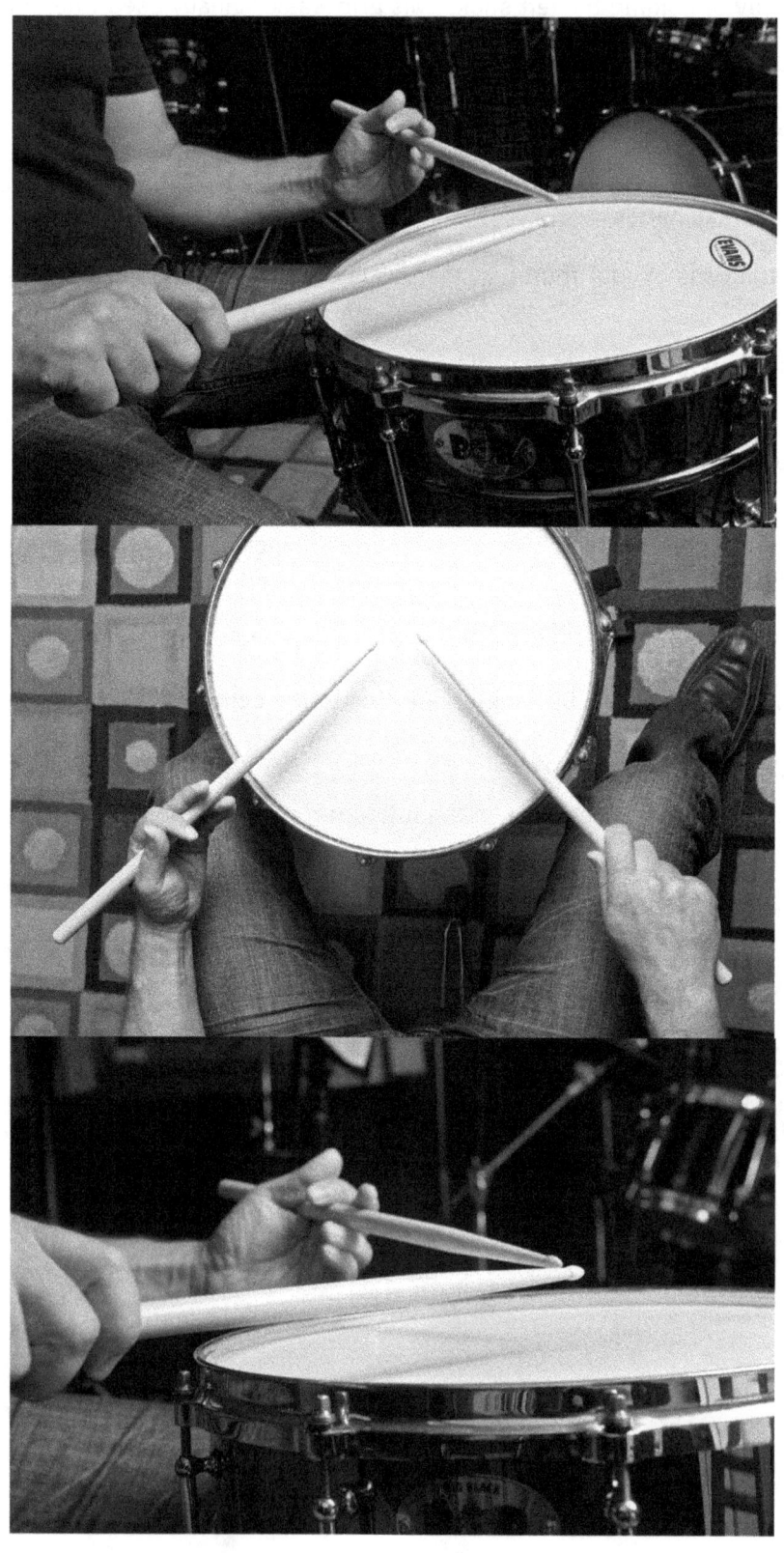

Music Notation 1: Introducing Quarter Notes

In my 20 plus years of teaching drums, I have learned that many people are afraid to read music. WHY? Because they think it is hard. They will sometimes say it is because they want to feel the music and reading will make it like math or something. The best drummers do both! Most of the drummers that you hear on recordings, including the ones with the best feel and groove, read music. If you can count to four then reading music will be easy for you.

Below is a staff in a bar or measure. The staff is the horizontal lines and spaces. The bar or measure is the space between the bar lines.

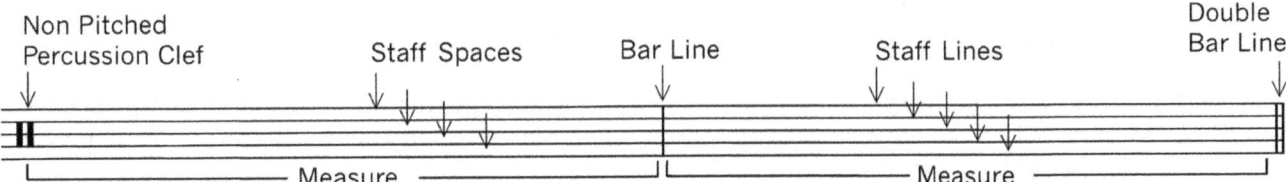

Quarter notes are counted 1 2 3 4 with even space between each count. Below you will see quarter notes written within a staff. There are four evenly spaced quarter note counts that will keep repeating in the bar below. The repeat sign tells you to go back to the beginning repeat sign. The area between the repeat signs is called a bar or a measure.

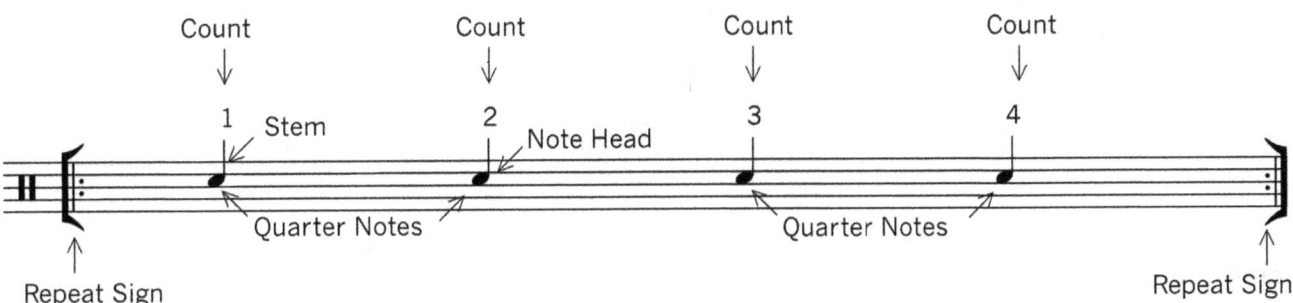

Time Signature

Time signature tells you how many beats are in a measure or bar and what type of note equals one beat. **The top number tells you how many beats per bar**. The top number 4 in the bar below tells you there are 4 beats in the bar. **The bottom number tells you which type of note equals one beat**. The 4 in the example below tells you a quarter note equals one beat.

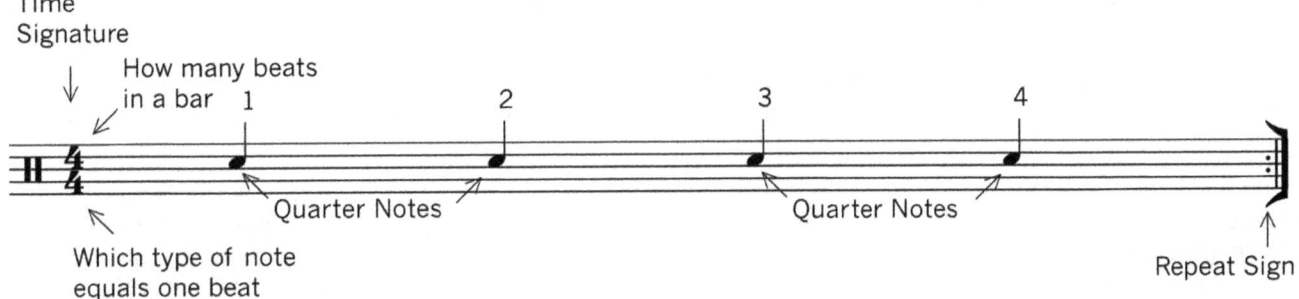

Half / Tap Stroke

A half / tap stroke is when you drop the stick from the start position and let it bounce back to the start position. When practicing this stroke you should multitask and be aware if you are using all the previous grip ideas as you play.

1. Place your sticks in "Start Position" 3–5 inches off the drum.

2. From start position, throw the stick down with your wrist and let the stick bounce up like a ball and return to the start position.

3. When the stick bounces to the start position, gently close your fingers and stick to your palm to prevent the stick from rebounding higher than the start position.

4. To perform this correctly, the stick must come back to the start position BY ITSELF. DO NOT LIFT THE STICK! LET IT BOUNCE! There is a completely different feel when you lift or pull the stick up as opposed to letting it bounce back up.

Exercise: Half / Tap Stroke

Now practice the half stroke with the music below. Play each hand individually until you see and feel each stroke returning the same back to the start position. It should return without you lifting it back to the start position.

Play from the start position and let each stroke return. Count out loud as you play.

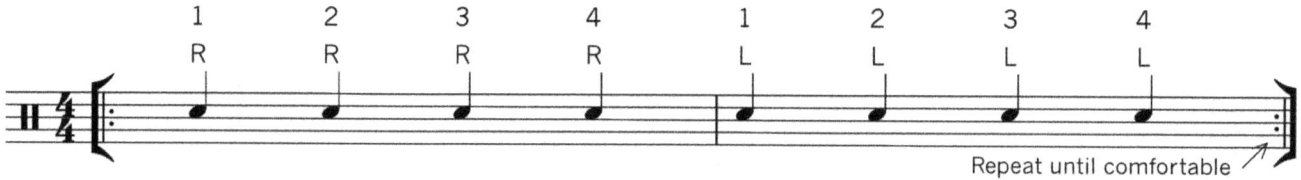

You will probably find that one hand is more comfortable than the other. Spend more time on the less comfortable hand.

Introducing the Metronome to Half / Tap Strokes

Now that you have mastered each hand individually, try 4 rights and 4 lefts with a metronome. Tap your right foot with the metronome.

Play from the start position and let each stroke return. Count out loud as you play.

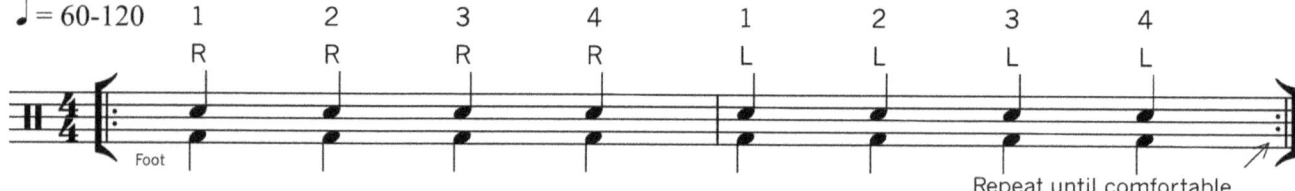

ALWAYS START SLOWLY! Set your metronome to a slow tempo 60–70 beats per minute and practice making each stroke match the metronome's tempo. Speed should be the last thing you are concerned with.

Make each stroke sound the same. Make each bounce stroke look the same: if they look the same they will sound the same. In other words, each stick should be the same height and have matching motion. There should be no difference in sound or spacing between any right or left! When you can do all the above for a few minutes, gradually increase the speed of the metronome (5 beats per minute at the most). Lock into that tempo for a few minutes and then repeat going faster.

Full Stroke

A full stroke starts at the start position just like a ½ stroke. From the start position lift the stick by doing an up stroke until it points at the ceiling. For softer full strokes do not lift the stick as high. **When you throw down the stick it should return to the start position for every stroke.** This is the stroke to use when you play an accented or loud note followed by an unaccented note.

Exercise: Full Strokes Practice 4 rights and 4 lefts making all full strokes sound the same. Use a metronome.

From the start position lift the stick to the full sroke postion by doing an up stroke, then throw each stroke down and make each stroke return to and stop at the start position.

Full / Rebound Stroke

A full rebound stroke is when you start with the stick pointing to the ceiling and drop the stick letting it bounce back to the same height as you started. (Note that the half stroke on the previous page only bounces up to the start position.) For softer full rebound stroke volumes you can start closer to the drum and let the stick bounce back to the same height as you started.

1. Set yourself so that your sticks are pointing up at the ceiling with your fingers closed on the sticks and wrists bent back.

2. Your elbows should be relaxed at your sides and your forearm should be flat from your elbow to your wrist.

3. With the tips of your sticks pointing at the ceiling, throw the stick down to the drum letting the stick rebound up BY ITSELF so that the tip of your stick points back up at the ceiling.

4. **WRIST REBOUND: Practice this rebound first.** When the stick bounces up, your wrist should follow the stick up and point at the ceiling.

5. **Finger Rebound: Practice this rebound second.** Your fingers should open up away from the palm to allow the stick to rebound up and point towards the ceiling or "12 o'clock," "11 o'clock" is fine also. As you go faster, the rebound can get closer to the drum.

6. Practice each hand individually until you feel and see each stroke rebounding up on its own like a ball. YOU DO THE DOWN MOTION; THE STICK DOES THE UP MOTION.

Exercise: Rebound Strokes Practice first as wrist rebounds, then as finger rebounds. Use a metronome.

Play from the full stroke position and let each stroke return.

Music Notation 2: Introducing 8th Notes

8th notes are twice as fast as quarter notes. 8th notes are counted like this: 1 and 2 and 3 and 4 and. I will abbreviate the "and" count with a "+" which will look like this: 1 + 2 + 3 + 4 + (see the count above the notes in the example below).

8th notes look like this:

    8th notes with flags   8th notes beamed together with bars

Introducing the Metronome to Rebound Strokes

Now that you have mastered each hand individually try 8 rights and 8 lefts. The metronome will be set to quarter notes and will click on every number count. See the example below. Notice how the quarter note in the bottom space lines up with every number count.

Exercise: 8 Rights and 8 Lefts Rebound 8th Notes

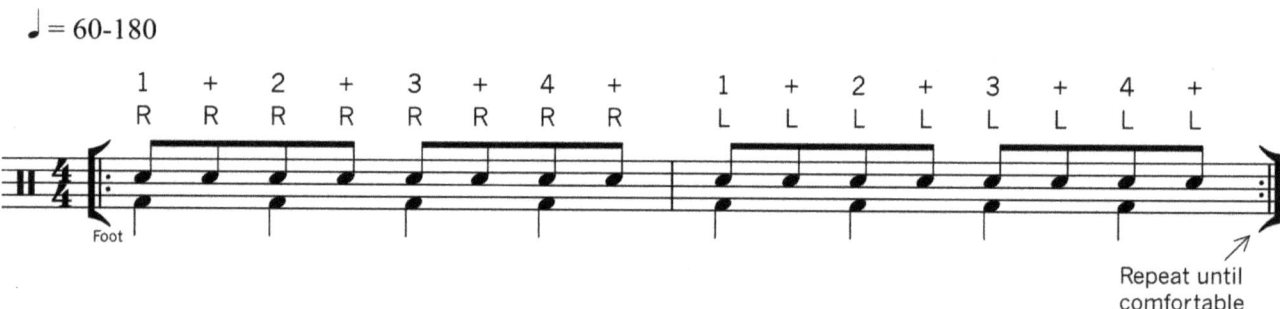

ALWAYS START SLOWLY! Set your metronome to a slow tempo 60–70 beats per minute and practice making each stroke match the metronome's tempo. When you add your foot it will tap with the metronome on all quarter notes and number counts.

Make all notes sound the same. Make each rebound stroke look the same: if they look the same they will sound the same. In other words each stick should be the same height and have matching motion. There should be no difference in sound or spacing between any right or left! When you can do all the above for a few minutes, gradually increase the speed of the metronome (5 beats per minute at the most). Lock into that tempo for a few minutes, and then repeat going faster.

Introducing Rudiments

There are four families of rudiments:

1. Rolls
2. Diddles
3. Flams
4. Drags

Why learn rudiments? When you learn rudiments correctly they will help you have the techniques that you want and need to be a successful drummer. Without them, you will eventually wonder why you can't do certain things that you hear other drummers doing. Rudiments will help give you the techniques you need for every style of music.

Single Stroke Roll

Single strokes are played just like full / rebound strokes. Now, just put one hand in between the other.

1. When playing single strokes let **every** stroke rebound the same.

2. Every note should rebound to the same height (right and left the same).

3. If they look the same they will sound the same. *Same height + Same motion = Same sound*

4. Practice slowly at first at your own pace.

5. Also practice single strokes as half (tap) strokes.

Introducing the Metronome to Single Strokes

Now that you have mastered single strokes at your own tempo, add the metronome.

ALWAYS START SLOWLY! Set your metronome to a slow tempo 60–70 beats per minute and practice making each stroke match the metronome's tempo.

As before, make all notes sound the same. Make each single stroke look the same: if they look the same they will sound the same. In other words, each stick should be the same height and have matching motion. There should be no difference in sound or spacing between any right or left! When you can do all the above exercises **for a few minutes consistently**, gradually increase the speed of the metronome (5 beats per minute at the most). Lock into that tempo for a few minutes, and then repeat going faster.

Double Stroke Roll

Double stroke rolls are also called open rolls, corps or military style rolls. Double strokes combine a full / rebound for the first stroke and a full stroke for the second note. The rebound or full stroke is what happens after the stick hits the drum.

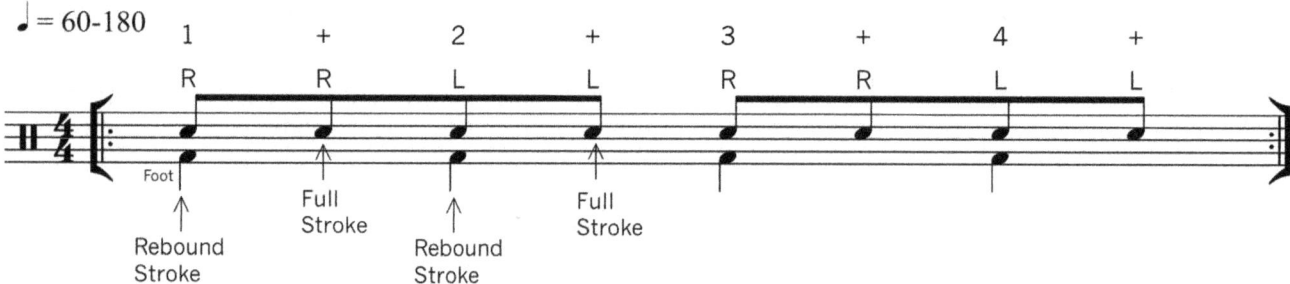

1. The 1st stroke is a full / rebound stroke. **The rebound is the most important part of double strokes. If the 1st stroke does not rebound the second stroke will not sound the same**. From the start position do an up stroke to the full position, drop the stick to the drum with your wrist letting the first stroke rebound your fingers open. Your wrist should not rebound up with the stick. Your fingers should open to let the stick up.

2. The 2nd stroke is a full stroke. The stick should be pointing up in the full stroke position after the first stroke has rebounded. Close your fingers to your palm to play the second stroke. This should bring the stick back to the start position.

3. Practice with each hand individually. You may need to spend more time on your weaker hand.

4. Practice alternating between hands. Play at an even tempo with no difference in sound or spacing.

Add the Metronome to Double Strokes

Use guidelines as before. Make sure to use the double stroke ideas above. As you increase the speed your sticks can be closer to the drum.

Multiple Bounce Stroke Roll

Multiple bounce stroke rolls are also called buzz rolls, closed rolls, or orchestral style rolls.

1. From the start position drop the stick to the drum keeping it on the drumhead lightly, letting it make a buzz sound as soon as it hits the drum. The stick should not bounce then buzz—it should buzz immediately.

2. Practice one hand at a time. As usual, one hand will be less comfortable. Work more on the less comfortable hand.

3. Switch from right to left **slowly** trying to let the stick sustain into the next stroke.

4. Listen for a consistent sound from hand to hand.

5. Keep the same tempo for single strokes and buzz strokes. Use a metronome and start slowly.

6. Your sticks should be close to the drum when playing Multiple Bounce Strokes. Your sticks will not make a buzz sound if they are not on the drumhead.

Add the Metronome

Going forward, you should be able to play everything in tempo with a metronome. Use guidelines as before and add the metronome to all the exercises in this book. You will notice that the metronome markings above the exercises are a range of tempos. You should always start slowly and practice until you are comfortable before increasing the speed.

Paradiddles

Paradiddles are a combination of single strokes and double strokes with an accent or louder note on the first stroke. Paradiddles require correct and consistent stick heights to be played correctly. The stick height is what is used to play louder or softer notes. Hitting harder or softer does not work as efficiently.

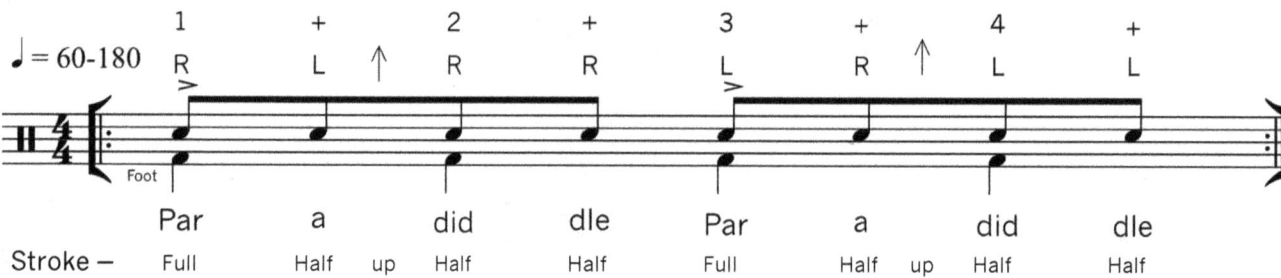

1. Begin with sticks in the start position.

2. Keep left hand still at start position. Raise right stick, which is called a "prep" or "up" stroke to the full stroke position using your wrist. (This will naturally create the accent by dropping the stick from a higher level.)

3. Drop the right stick to the drum letting it bounce back to the start position. This is NOT a rebound stroke. It is a full stroke that returns to the start position. You can achieve keeping the stick at the start position by closing your fingers after you strike the drum.

4. From the start position drop the left stick to the drum to play the second note and then raise it to the full stroke position to prepare for the next accent, this is called an up stroke.

5. Drop the next two right strokes from the start position without raising them first. The only up stroke is for the accented note; no other note should be raised above the start position.

I recommend playing the Paradiddle and *almost* all other rudiments with accents from 2 stick heights:

1. Start position 3–5 inches off drum for unaccented notes.

2. Accent position 7–12 inches for the accented notes or "11" or "12" o'clock.
No need to use a ruler—just be consistent. The stick height is what you should use to change the volume. Play closer to drum for softer notes, higher off the drum for louder notes. You should adjust the height as you need to play the music louder or softer.

Flams

Flams are two strokes: a half stroke and a full stroke played at "almost" the same time. The half stroke, which is the small note below is called a grace note and gets no time value in music. The grace note is a "decorative" or "ornamental" note.

1. Start with both hands at start position.

2. Keep left hand still at start position. Raise right stick using your wrist (up stroke) to the full stroke position.

3. Drop both sticks from this position to the drum and let them bounce back to start position.

4. Now the opposite hand. Keep right hand still at start position, raise the left hand with wrist.

5. Drop the stick to the drum letting the stick bounce back to the start position.

6. Keep alternating slowly, trying to get a consistent "FLA" sound.

7. Beware of "Flat" flams. This is when the sticks hit at the same time.

8. Beware of the strokes being too far apart.

Correct stick height and position is the key to playing good flams. Do not try to force your flams. Relax the sticks down to the drum.

Drags

Drags are three notes: two grace notes (double strokes) played as half strokes, and one main note played as a full stroke with the opposite hand.

Practice the double stroke grace notes first. Listen for 2 even grace notes from the half stroke position.

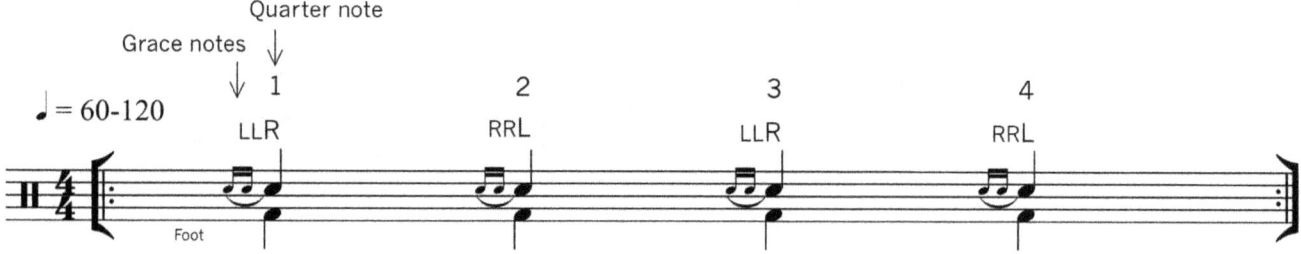

1. Start with both hands at start position.

2. Raise right stick with wrist several inches above start position (prep stroke) to the full stroke position.

3. Drop left hand from start position letting it bounce twice. The right hand should drop immediately after, creating three notes hitting the drum almost together.

4. All three notes should be articulated. There should NOT be a buzz sound. The drag should sound like two soft double strokes and a main note.

5. Rhythmically, drags are counted as the main note. For instance, in the example above count quarter notes. It is important to understand that the grace notes do not receive value in the rhythm—they just "fatten" it up. Think of grace notes as decorations on the main note.

Music Notation 3: Introducing 16th Notes

16th notes are twice as fast as 8th notes and 4 times as fast as quarter notes.

16th notes look like this:

16th notes are counted like this: 1 e and a 2 e and a 3 e and a 4 e and a. I will abbreviate the "and" count with a "+" which will look like this: 1 e + a 2 e + a 3 e + a 4 e + a (see the count above the notes in the example above).

Exercise: Single Stroke 16th Notes
Use all grip and technique ideas as before. Play Single Stroke 16th notes as Full / Rebound strokes and Half / Tap Strokes. Stick height will depend on speed and volume.

The metronome will be set to quarter notes and will click on every number count. See the example above. Notice the quarter note on the bottom space lines up with the number count.

Exercise: Double Stroke 16th Notes
Use all grip and technique ideas as before. Play the first note of each Double Stroke 16th note as a Full / Rebound stroke and the second note as a Half / Tap Stroke. Stick height will depend on speed and volume.

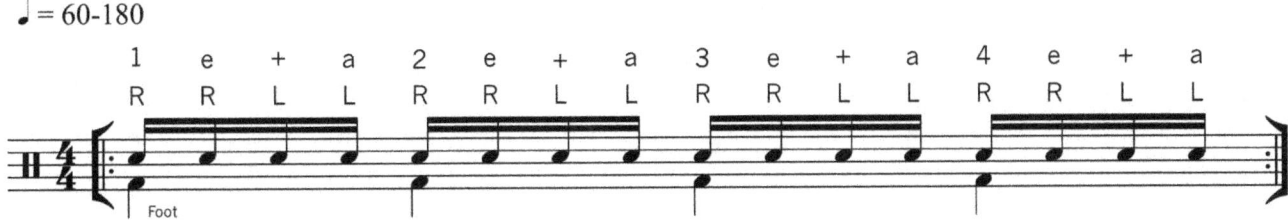

Basic Technique and Rudiment Exercises 1

1. Half / Tap Stroke Quarter Notes
Play from the start position: 3-5 inches off the drum. Let each stroke return to the start position.
Count out loud as you play.

2. Full / Rebound Stroke Quarter Notes
Play from the full position: 6-12 inches off the drum. Let each stroke return to the full position.

3. 8 Rights and 8 Lefts Rebound 8th Notes
When counting 8th notes "+" is pronounced "and."

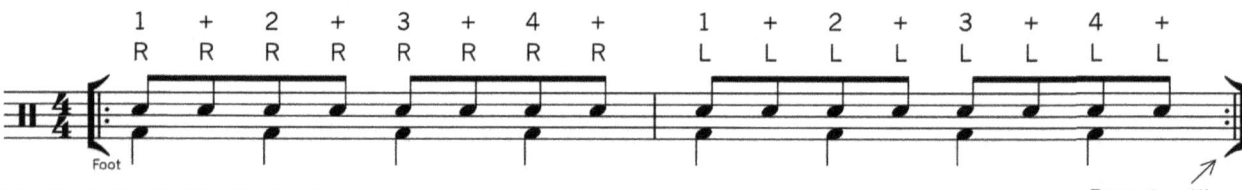

4. Single Stroke 8th Notes
Single Strokes should be played as rebound strokes and tap strokes.

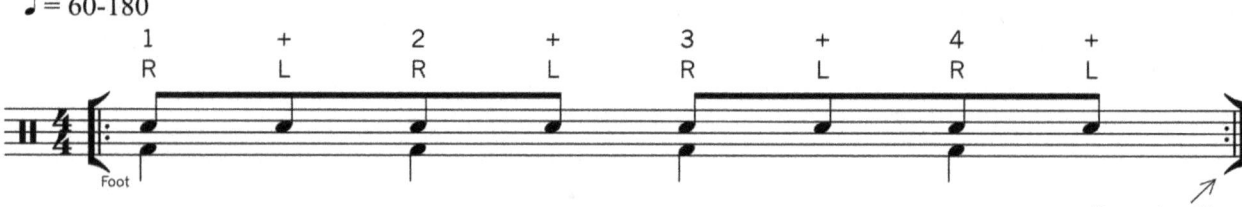

5. Single Stroke 16th Notes

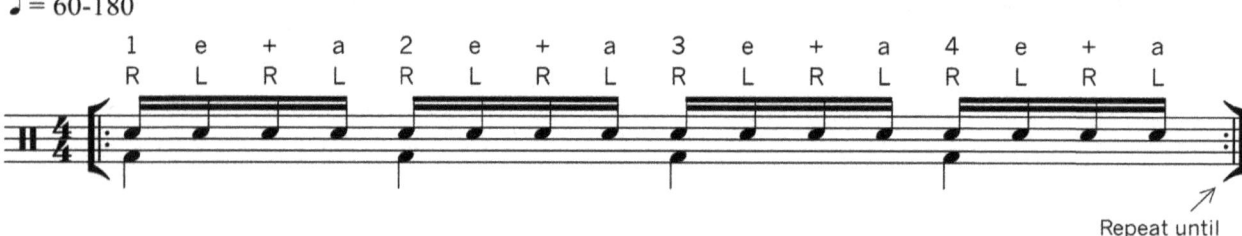

Basic Technique and Rudiment Exercises 2

Basic Technique and Sticking Excercises

♩ = 60-180

Rebound / Full Strokes — Half / Tap Strokes

1 R R R R L L L L | R R R R L L L L
f (forte = loud) — *p (piano = soft)*
(Foot)

2 R R R R R L R L R L R L

3 L L L L L R L R L R L R

4 R R L L R L R L R R L L R L R L

5 L L R R L R L R L L R R L R L R

6 R L R L R L R L R L R L R L R L | R R L L R R L L R R L L R R L L

7 L L R R L L R R L L R R L L R R | L R L R L R L R L R L R L R L R

When you are comfortable tapping your right foot on quarter notes add your left foot on counts 2 & 4.

20 Introduction to Basics   Scott Strunk

Part 2: Reading Rhythms

As you begin this section, **AWARENESS** will be the key to your success. If you can answer yes to the 3 questions below as you are playing, you have got it. If not, you do not have it!

I will list the 3 questions in order of priority. Ask yourself these questions as you play *after* you can count and play the exercise.

1. Can I count the rhythm in tempo without playing?
2. Can I play the rhythm correctly while counting in tempo?
3. Do I sound even and is the balance of volumes between sticks the same?

"When in doubt, count it out!"
If you can count a rhythm, you can play it.
If you can't count a rhythm, you can't play it.

Reading Rhythms: Notes and Rests and Sub-Divisions

1st and 2nd endings: Play from the beginning to the repeat sign at the end of the first ending. Repeat back to the beginning. On the second time through skip the 1st ending and go right to the 2nd ending.

4 Bar Note and Rest Combinations 1

Add dynamics as marked below the lines. *f = forte = loud p = piano = soft*. For a list of other common dynamic markings and their meaning, see the music terminology page in the appendix of this book.

4 Bar Note and Rest Combinations 2

24 Reading Rhythms   Scott Strunk

4 Bar Note and Rest Combinations 3

8th and 16th Notes Connected 1

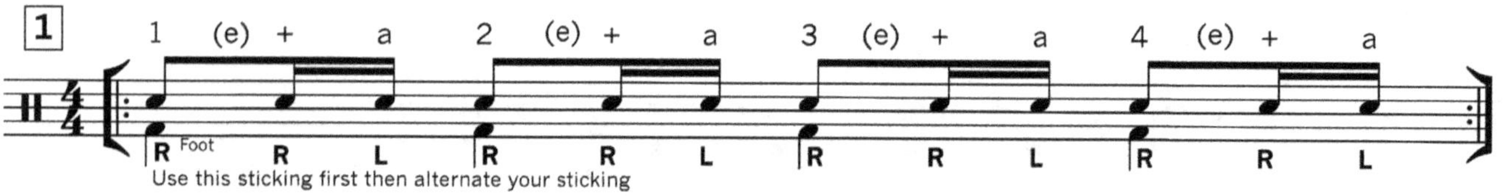

26 Reading Rhythms Scott Strunk

8th and 16th Notes Connected 2

Dotted Notes and Ties

Dotted Notes and Rests: A dot adds 1/2 the value of the note or rest to the note or rest.

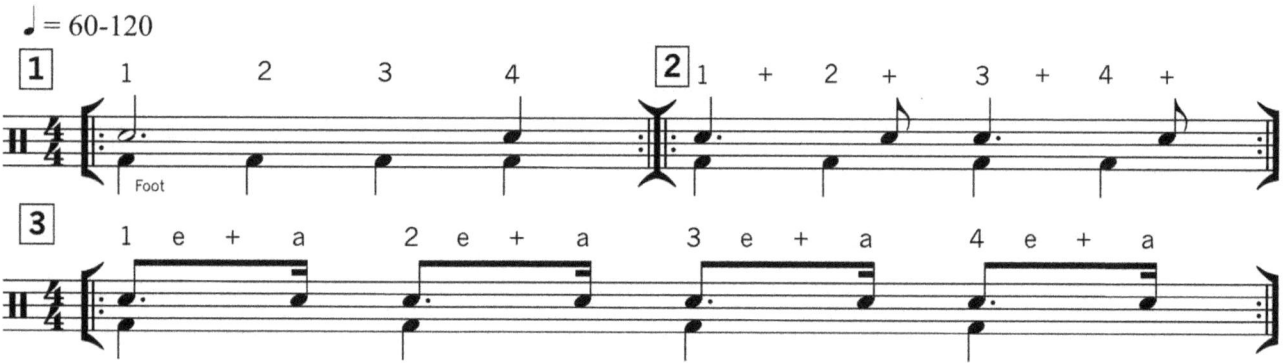

Tied Notes: A tie makes a note hold through the note to which it is tied. You don't play the note at the end of the tie.

Combination Exercise

28   Reading Rhythms   Scott Strunk

Subdivisions with 8th and 16th Triplets

8th note triplets are three equally spaced notes per beat. 16th note triplets are six equally spaced notes per beat. 16th note triplets are twice as fast as 8th note triplets.

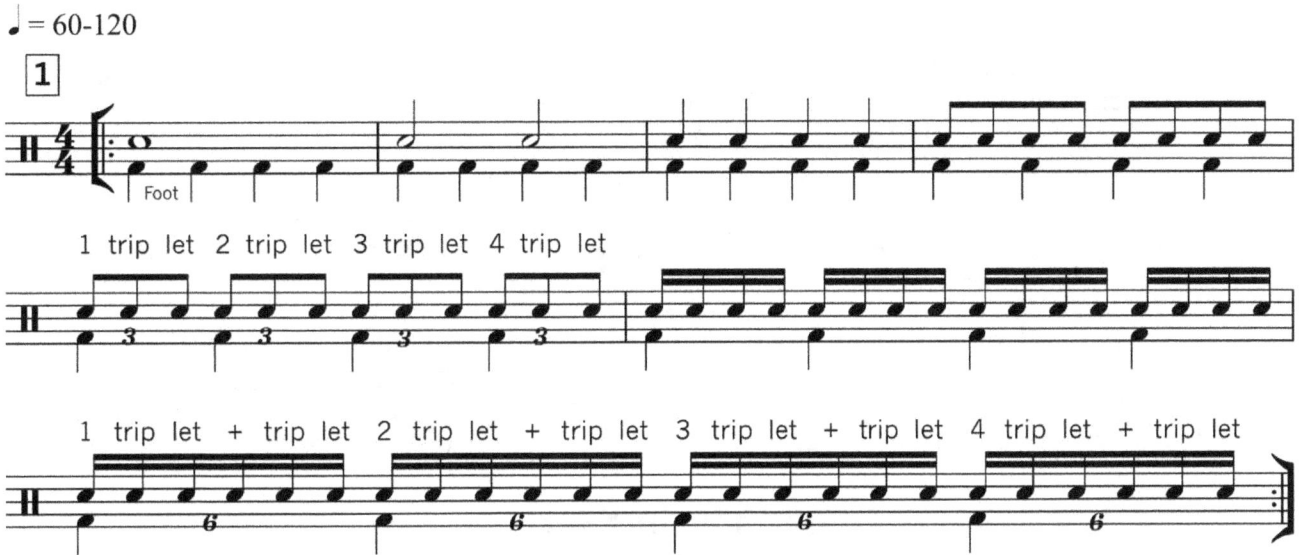

Subdivisions with 1/2 and 1/4 Note Triplets

A half-note triplet is when you play on every other note of a quarter note triplet. A quarter note triplet is when you play on every other note of an 8th note triplet.

Quarter and 8th Note Triplet Exercises

30   Reading Rhythms   Scott Strunk

Syncopation 1

Syncopation is when music is written in a way that places the emphasis on a weak beat instead of a strong beat. For example, the emphasis would be on the up beat, or "and" count, instead of on the down beat or number count.

When reading syncopation it is important to think about the duration of the notes in addition to the attack.

Also try these exercises swinging the 8th notes. Swinging the 8th notes is when 8th note counts become triplet counts. The 8th note counts 1 + become 1 let. 1 let is the first and last count of a group of triplets. The trip count is left out.

Scott Strunk Reading Rhythms 31

Rolls in Rhythm 1

When rolling in rhythm always choose a subdivision to count while rolling. Count that subdivision from the beginning of the roll to the end. In most music it is best to count a 16th note subdivision when rolling. This will change for the tempo or feel of the music, or when asked to play a specific length roll.

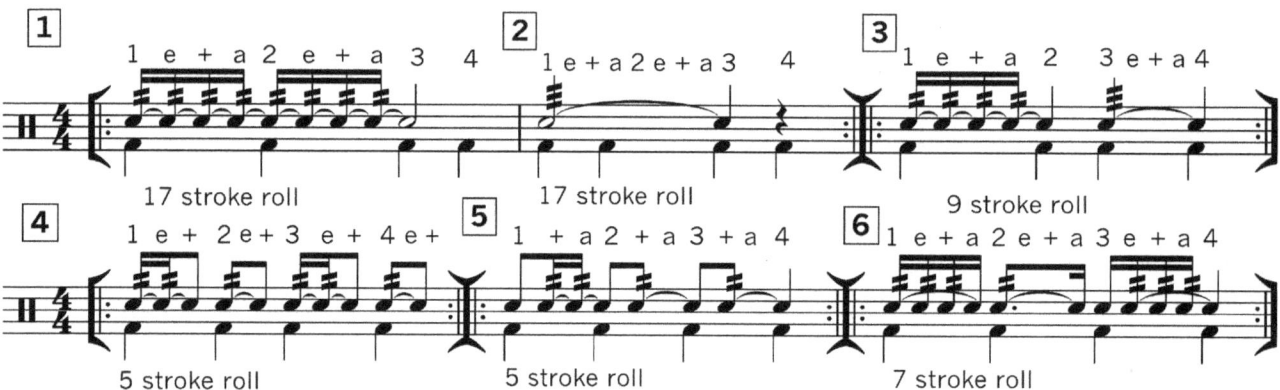

If you have trouble figuring out how to roll correctly answer these three questions: 1. What count does the roll start on? 2. What count does the roll end on ? 3. How do you count the subdivision in between the start and the end of the roll?

Combination Exercise

Practice playing all rolls Buzzed and Double Stroked.

32   Reading Rhythms   Scott Strunk

Rolls in Rhythm 2

Rolls in Triplets

For this piece, subdivide triplets as you roll to match the triplet feel of the music.

16th Note Triplet Exercises

34 Reading Rhythms Scott Strunk

Syncopation 2

Also try these exercises swinging the 8th and 16th notes. Swinging the 8th notes is when the counts 1 + become 1 let. Swinging the 16th notes is when counts 1 e + a become 1 let + let. The trip count or middle count of the triplet is left out.

Cut Time

Cut Time is also called "Alle Breve." This means that you count the music twice as fast as common time or 4/4. When playing in cut time you count in 2 instead of 4. The note and rest values are cut in 1/2. Quarter notes are counted as 8th notes and 8th notes are counted as 16th notes, etc.

Combination Exercise

For another challenging exercise play other pages from this book in Cut Time.

36   Reading Rhythms   Scott Strunk

6/8 Time Signature

The top number tells you that there are 6 beats in every bar. The bottom number tells you that an 8th note equals 1 beat. 6/8 time signature can be felt in 6 for slower tempos (see exercise #1 below.) 6/8 can also be felt in 2 for faster tempos (see exercise #2 below.)

Scott Strunk

Subdivisions Adding 5s, 7s, and 32nd Notes

I recommend practicing 5s, 7s, and 32nd notes repeatedly with a metronome before adding them to the subdivision exercise.

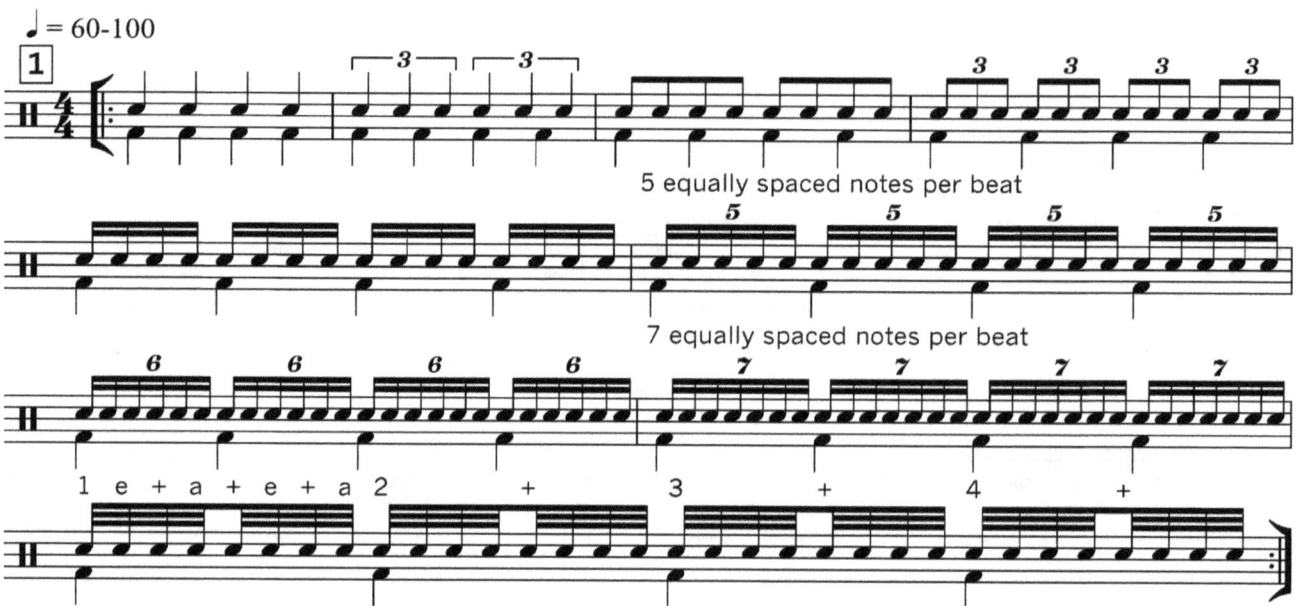

32nd notes are a group of 8 notes per beat and can be counted a couple of different ways depending on the tempo of the music:
1. Count 8th notes. There will be a group of 4 notes to every 8th note count for fast tempos.
2. Count 16th notes with the starting hand and there will be an alternate stroke in between.

Combination Exercise

*Fermata:
Hold the note until cut off.

38 Reading Rhythms   Scott Strunk

Exercises in Various Time Signatures 1

Exercises in Various Time Signatures 2

Part 3: The 40 Standard Snare Drum Rudiments and Technique Exercises

As you begin this section, AWARENESS will be the key to your success. If you can answer yes to the 3 questions below as you are playing, you have got it. If not, you do not have it!

I will list the 3 questions in order of priority. Ask yourself these questions as you play *after* you can count and play the exercise.

1. Am I playing the sticking and rhythm correctly in tempo?
2. Am I striking the drum with correct stick heights?
3. Is the balance of volumes between sticks the same?

The 40 Standard Snare Drum Rudiments
There are four families of rudiments: Rolls, Diddles, Flams, and Drags
Rudiment Family #1 Roll Rudiments

At first start slowly and listen for quality of sound, eveness, correct sticking and accents. Once you have achieved this, gradually change speed from slow to fast and then back to slow. You should also be able to play rudiments at a steady moderate tempo.

On the next couple of pages you will begin playing rudiments with accents. When playing all rudiments with accents, I recommend using two stick heights. The first stick height is the start position (2-3 inches off the drum) for the unaccented notes. The second stick height is higher (6-8 inches off the drum) for the accented notes. Your sticks should get closer to the drum for softer volumes and faster tempos.
* There is only one rudiment that should NOT be played using my two stick height rule, the Flamacue. The Flamacue should be played using three stick heights because the Flam is not accented.
1st stick height: Start position for all of the unaccentd notes.
2nd stick height: Half accent postion for the main notes of the Flam.
(You can not play both notes of Flams from the start position. This will produce FLAT sounding Flams.)
3rd stick height: Full accent position for the accented notes.

Rudiment Family #1 Roll Rudiments
D. Measured Rolls (Play all measured rolls multiple bounce and double stroke)

If you have trouble figuring out how to roll correctly answer these three questions: 1. What count does the roll start on? 2. What count does the roll end on? 3. How do you count the subdivision in between?

Scott Strunk   Rudiments and Technique Exercises   43

Rudiment Family #2 Diddle Rudiments

Before you begin, be sure to read and apply the instructions on stick heights on pages 14 and 42. If you are playing rudiments that have accents without applying proper stick heights, they will not sound correct!

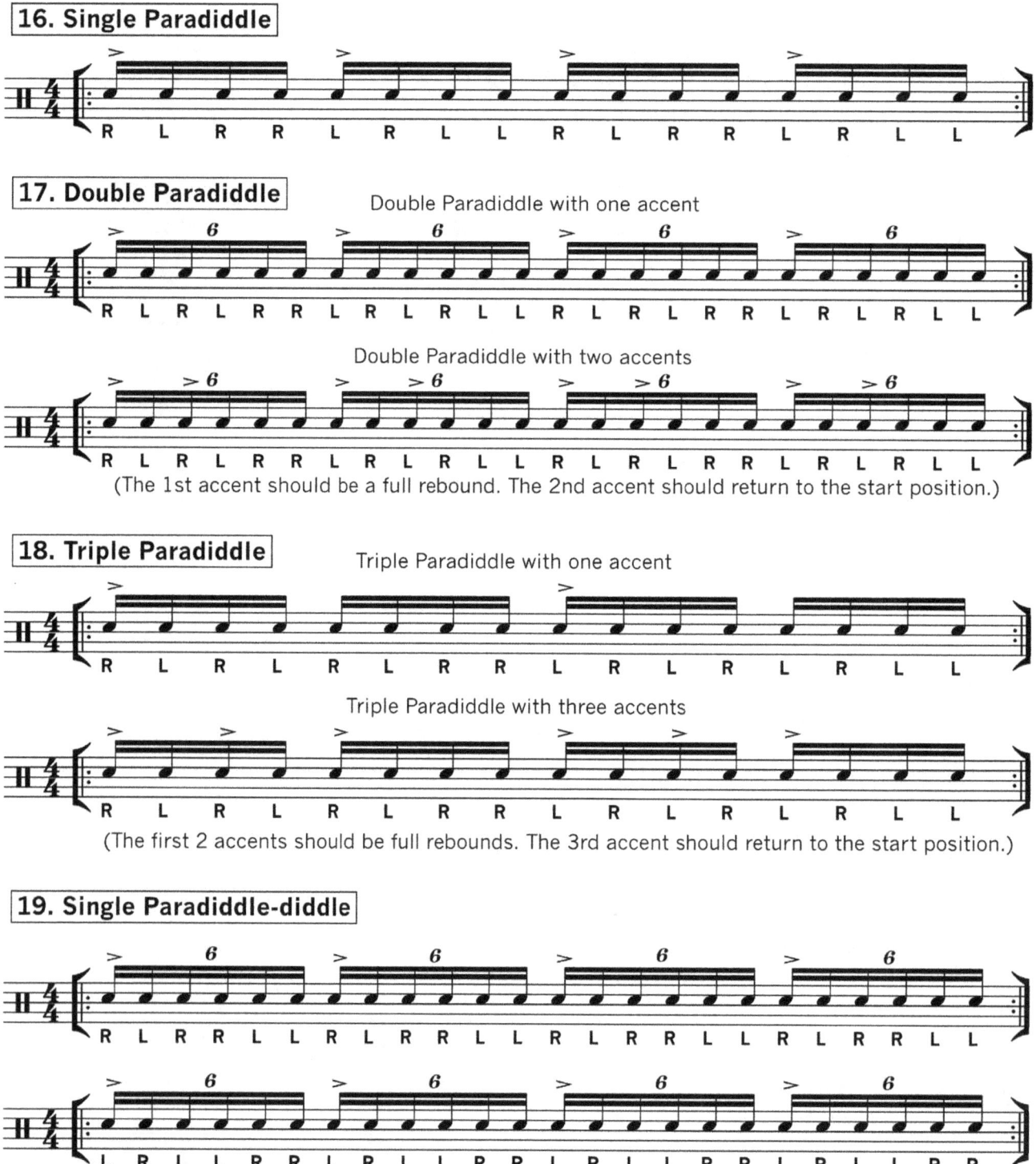

16. Single Paradiddle

17. Double Paradiddle
Double Paradiddle with one accent
Double Paradiddle with two accents
(The 1st accent should be a full rebound. The 2nd accent should return to the start position.)

18. Triple Paradiddle
Triple Paradiddle with one accent
Triple Paradiddle with three accents
(The first 2 accents should be full rebounds. The 3rd accent should return to the start position.)

19. Single Paradiddle-diddle

44 Rudiments and Technique Exercises Scott Strunk

Rudiment Family #3 Flam Rudiments

Rudiment Family #4 Drag Rudiments

46 Rudiments and Technique Exercises Scott Strunk

Sticking Exercises 1

Practice making all strokes sound the same. Play with and without repeats.
Repeat each exercise until you have evenness and comfort, then combine the exercises.

Tap right foot on all quarter note counts and left foot on counts 2 and 4. Also try this page in Cut Time.

Scott Strunk

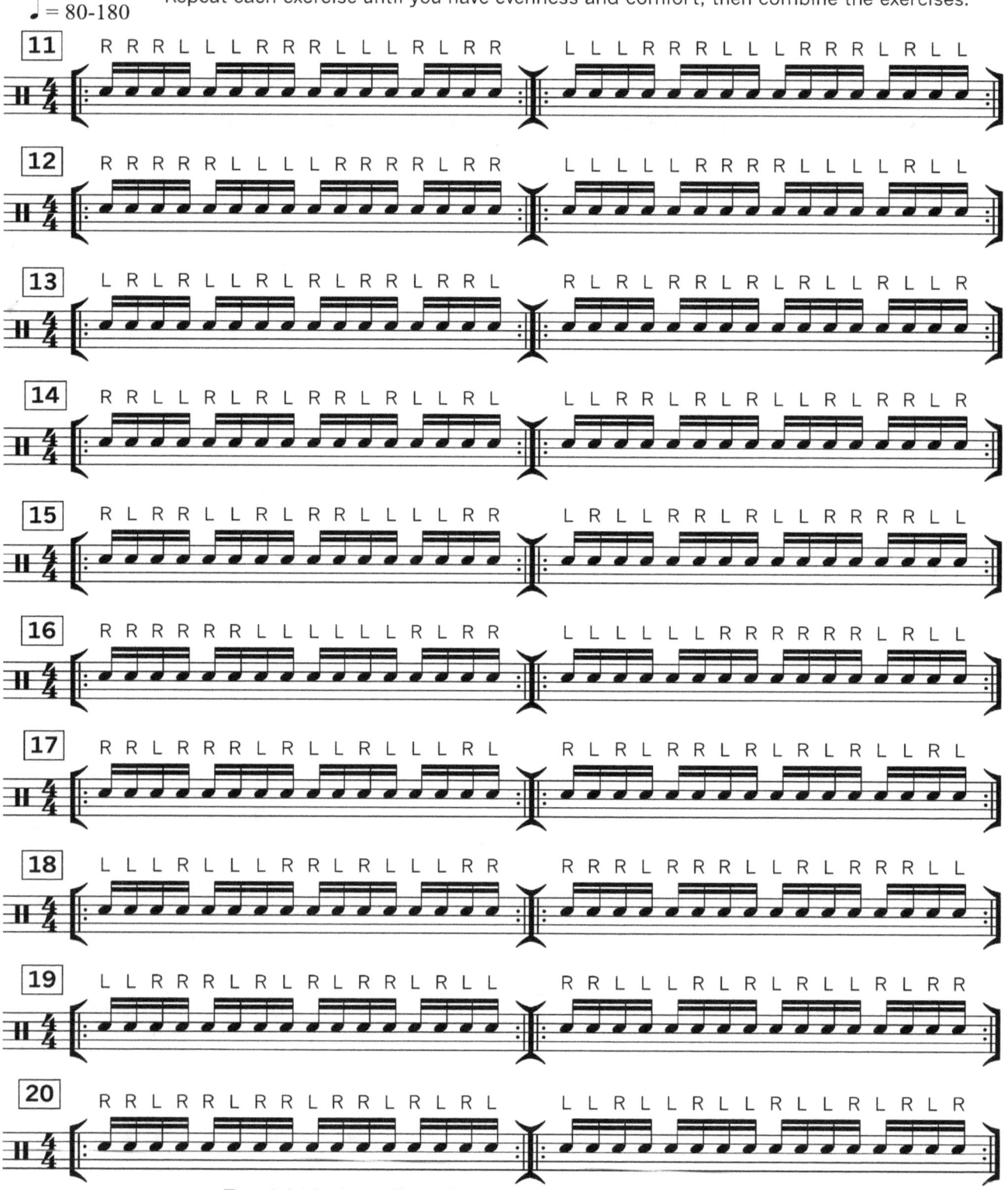

Accent Exercises 1

Play the next two pages with 2 stick heights: 1- Unaccented notes from start position 3 to 5 inches off the drum from the half / tap stroke position. 2- Accented notes 8 to 12 inches off the drum from the full stroke position. Your sticks should get closer to the drum as you get faster.

♩ = 80-180

1 Alternate strokes   Tap right foot on all quarter note counts and left foot on counts 2 and 4.

2 ♩ = 80-180

3 ♩ = 60-150

When you are able to play the exercises above comfortably, go back and play the unaccented notes as double strokes. When you double stroke an unaccented note, it will be double stroked twice as fast as the note written. Also try playing the accents as rimshots. Rimshots are when you hit the head and the rim of the drum at the same time.

Scott Strunk   Rudiments and Technique Exercises

Accent Exercises 2

♩ = 60-150 Tap right foot on all quarter note counts and left foot on counts 2 and 4.

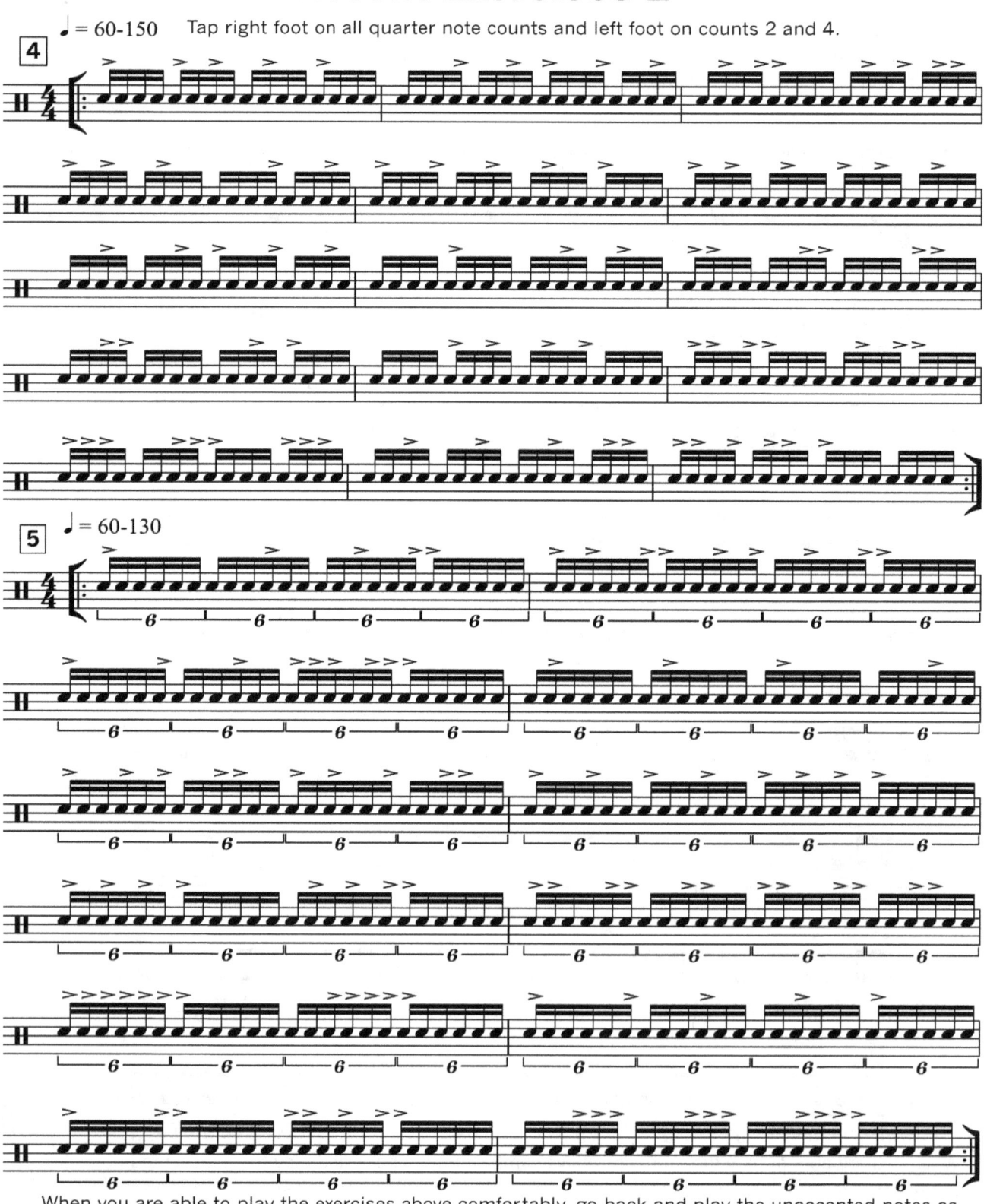

When you are able to play the exercises above comfortably, go back and play the unaccented notes as double strokes and play the accented notes as rimshots as listed on the previous page.

Rudiment Combos and Technique Exercises

♩ = 60-150

1. Single, Double, and Triple Stroke Triplet Combo

Tap right foot on all quarter note counts and left foot on 2 and 4.

♪ = 100-300

2. Flam Tap and Flam Accent Combo

♩ = 60-140

3. Flam Tap and Flam Accent Combo

Tap right foot on all quarter note counts and left foot on 2 and 4.

♪ = 100-180

4. Swiss Triplet and Flam Tap Combo

♩ = 60-130

5. Paradiddlediddle and Paradiddle Combo

Tap right foot on all quarter note counts and left foot on 2 and 4.

♩ = 60-130

6. Flam Paradiddle, Flam Tap, Flamacue, Swiss Triplet, and Flam Accent Combo

Tap right foot on all quarter note counts and left foot on 2 and 4.

Scott Strunk

Part 4: Drum Set Techniques, Coordination, Styles, Grooves, and Soloing

When learning drum set grooves and styles from any book, you must listen to great drummers in that style of music. You cannot learn how to play in a band from a book alone. Listen to and play along with great music...and play in bands yourself.

As you enter the drum set section, AWARENESS will be the key to your success. If you can answer the 3 questions below as you are playing, you have got it. If not, you do not have it!

I will list the 3 questions in order of priority. Ask yourself these questions as you play *after* you can count and play the exercise.

1. Am I playing the rhythms correctly in tempo?
2. Am I striking the drums and cymbals correctly?
3. Is the balance of volumes between all drums and cymbals correct?

Bass Drum and Hi-Hat Pedal Technique
There are 2 ways to play the Bass Drum and Hi-Hat pedal: Heel Down and Heel Up.

1. Heel Down- For softer strokes: place your foot flat on the pedal about two inches from the top or toe of the pedal. Throw with the top of your foot and pivot on your heel. Your toes and the ball of you foot always remain touching the pedal.

2. Heel Up- For louder strokes: pick up your heel about an inch or two. Your toes and the ball of your foot always remain touching the pedal about 2 inches from the top. Throw from your hip using your whole leg. Pivot on your hip and keep your ankle firm and relaxed.

Heel Down

Heel Up   Top View

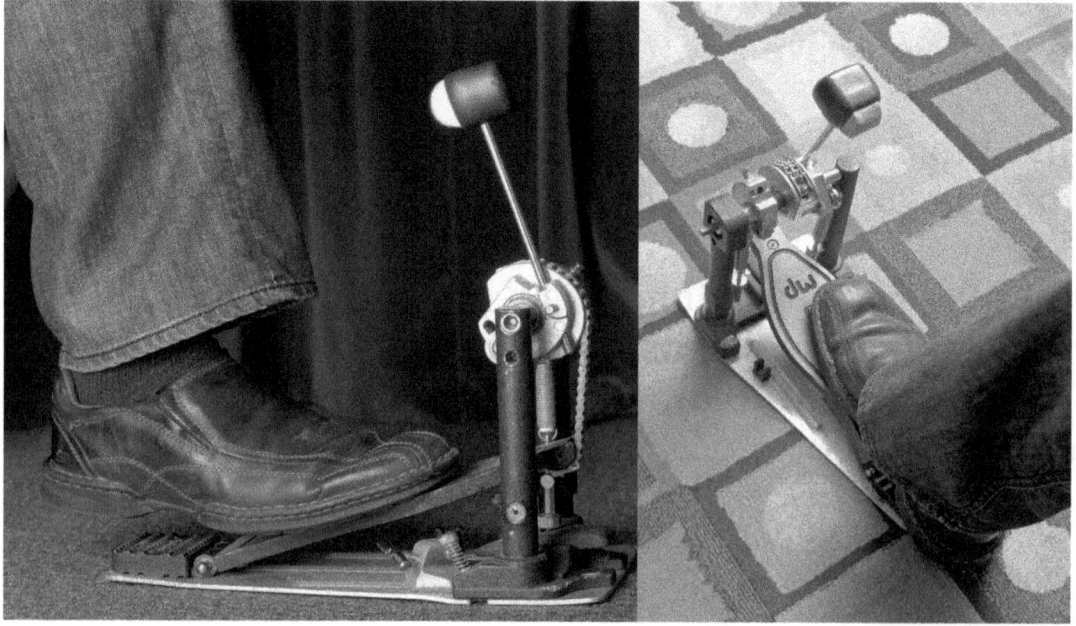

Basic Drum Set Coordination

You should be able to play with your foot heel up and heel down on the Bass Drum pedal. Let the beater bounce off the head just as you would a stick on a drum. For a different sound, you can choose to keep the beater on the head after you strike the Bass Drum, but this should not be used in all cicumstances.

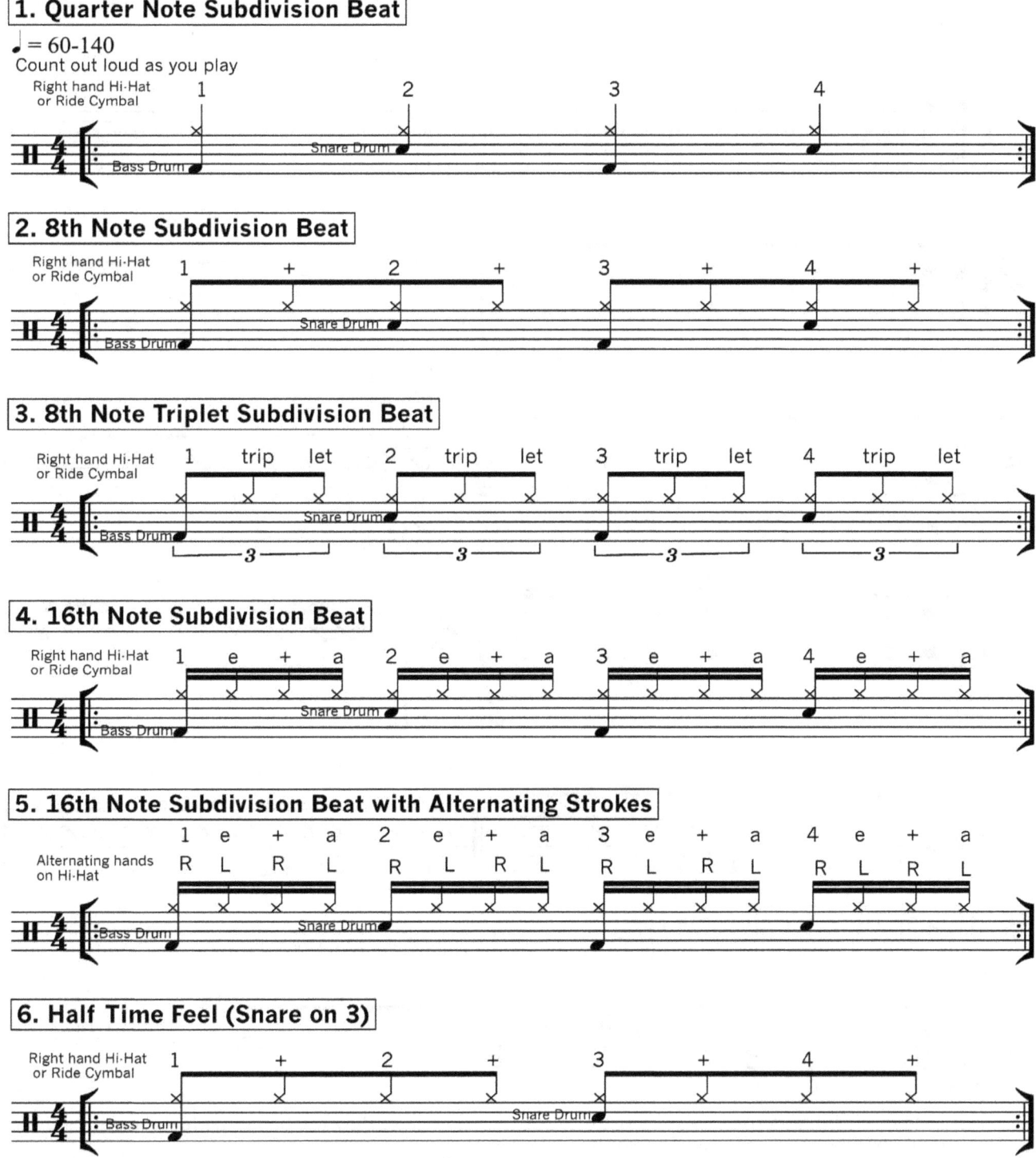

Scott Strunk

Basic Drum Set Coordination and Fills
Creating a 4 Bar Phrase

Play the same type of notes for the fill as you played for the beat. Use the whole drumset for the fill; be creative but stay in tempo.

Play regular time for 3 bars then fill for 1 bar into the half time feel. Play the half time feel for 3 bars then fill back to the beginning. This creates an 8 bar phrase.

Drum Set Coordination Exercises

The next six pages of Drum Set coordination exercises offer great ways of growing your vocabulary of beats, coordination, and understanding of reading music. Rather than just writing out hundreds of beats, I have given you many ways of combining hand patterns with foot patterns. You can mix all the patterns together and have unlimited beats! These types of patterns and combinations are used in Rock, Funk, and Fusion music.

Instructions for the Upcoming Drum Set Coordination Exercises

1. **Notice on every page that I have given a broad range of tempos in the metronome marking. Always choose a slow tempo first, then gradually increase the tempo. The metronome marking is just a guide for a tempo range.**

2. **Start by playing and repeating the hand patterns on the Hi-Hats and Snare one at a time.**

3. **Add a Bass Drum pattern one at a time to the hand pattern and repeat until locked in for a few minutes.**

4. **Play one Bass Drum pattern at a time and lock comfortably and consistently into the tempo.**

5. **Play heel up and heel down on the Bass Drum.**

6. **While playing a consistent hand pattern, play each Bass Drum pattern in a 2 and 4 bar phrase.**

7. **Move to the Ride Cymbal and add the Hi-Hat with your left foot, repeat as above.**

8. **When you have mastered this at a slow tempo, try a medium and fast tempo.**

9. **Play piano, mezzo forte, and forte.**

10. **Use your imagination and combine patterns and make your own beats.**

11. **Play the open Hi-Hat and pulsations hand parts on pages 61-62 with all the other pages of Bass Drum patterns.**

Use the 6 bars below to create and write your own beats and fills. Have Fun!

Quarter, 8th, and 16th Note Drum Set Coordination

8th and 16th Note Drum Set Coordination 1

8th and 16th Note Drum Set Coordination 2

♩ = 60-150

Hand Patterns

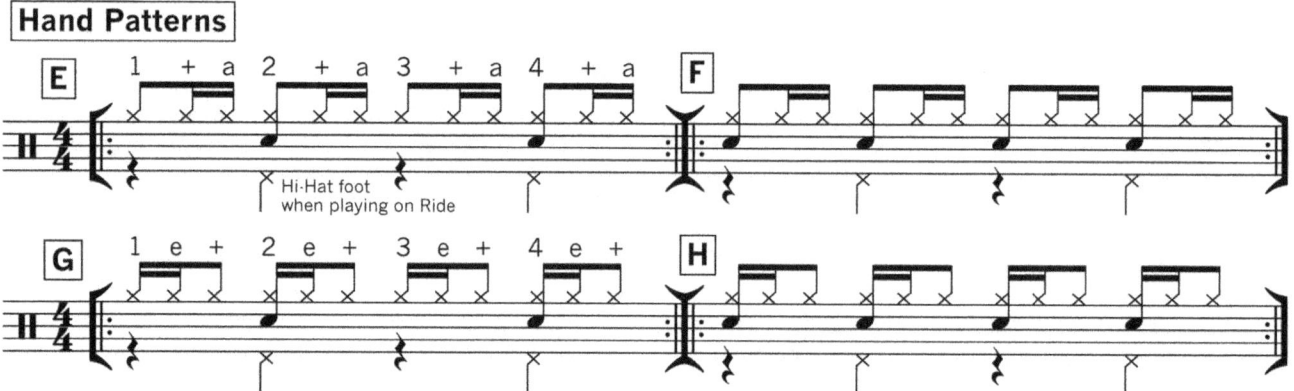

Practice right hand and left hand on the Hi-Hat. Also try alternating strokes on the Hi-Hat and bring the hand that plays on the Snare counts off the Hi-Hat to the Snare.

Bass Drum Patterns

Scott Strunk

Drum Set Coordination with 8th Note Pulsations and Open Hi-Hat

♩ = 60-150

Hand Patterns

Accented notes should be thought of as pulsations more than accents. Make a stronger, slight movement to the right to achieve a pulsation, rather than lifting the stick up like you would for an accent. When playing on the Ride Cymbal you can pulsate just like on the Hi-Hat, or play the accent on the bell.

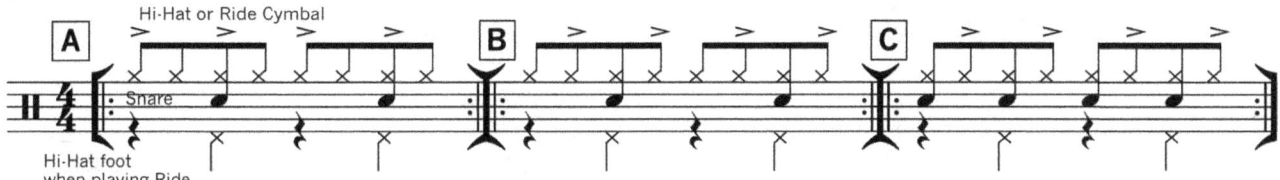

Open Hi-Hat Instructions: 1- Lift your foot just enough to separate the cymbals slightly. 2- Be definite when you close the Hi-Hat and make sure to close them on the correct beat. 3- Make sure not to flam if you are supposed to close and hit the Hi-Hat at the same time.

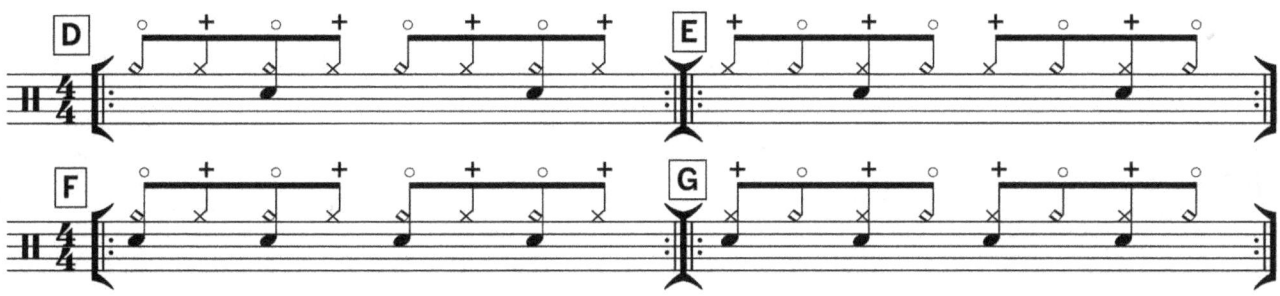

Bass Drum Patterns

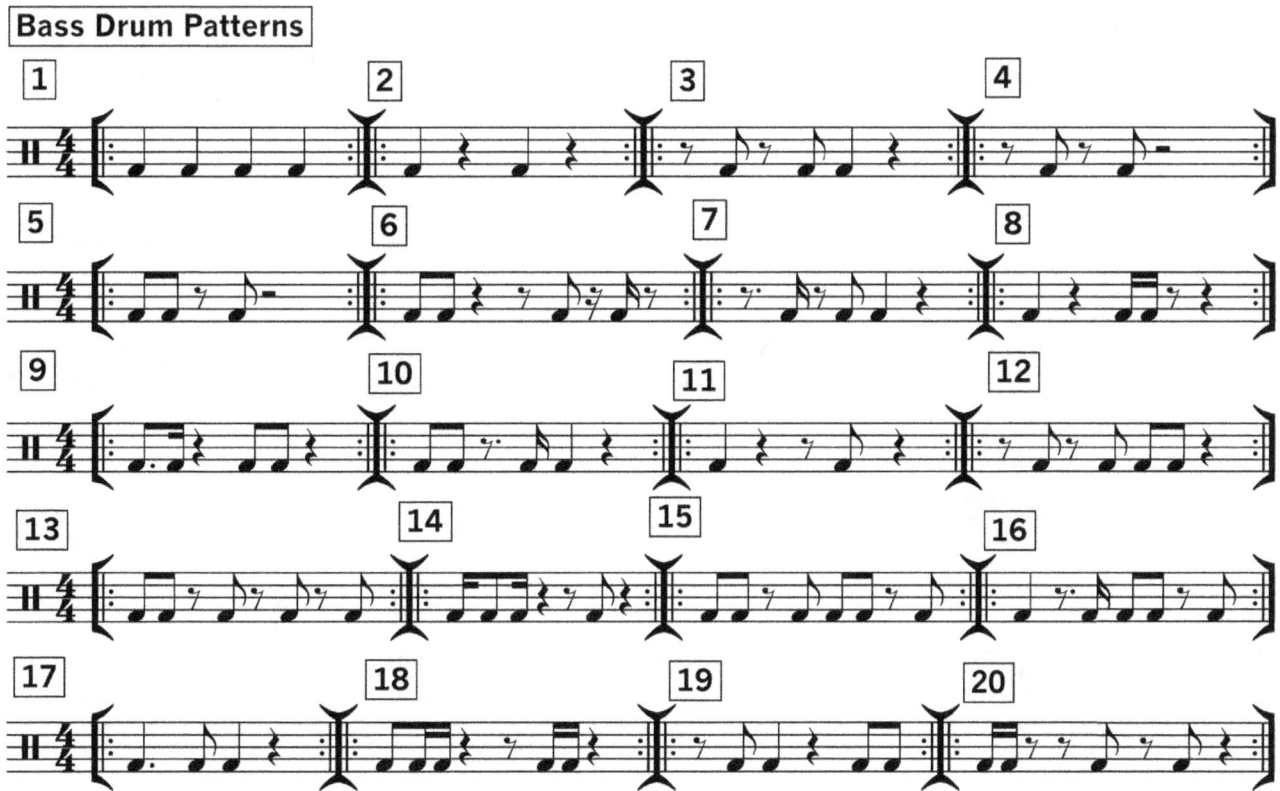

Scott Strunk

Drum Set   61

Drum Set Coordination with 16th Note Pulsations and Open Hi-Hat

♩ = 60-150

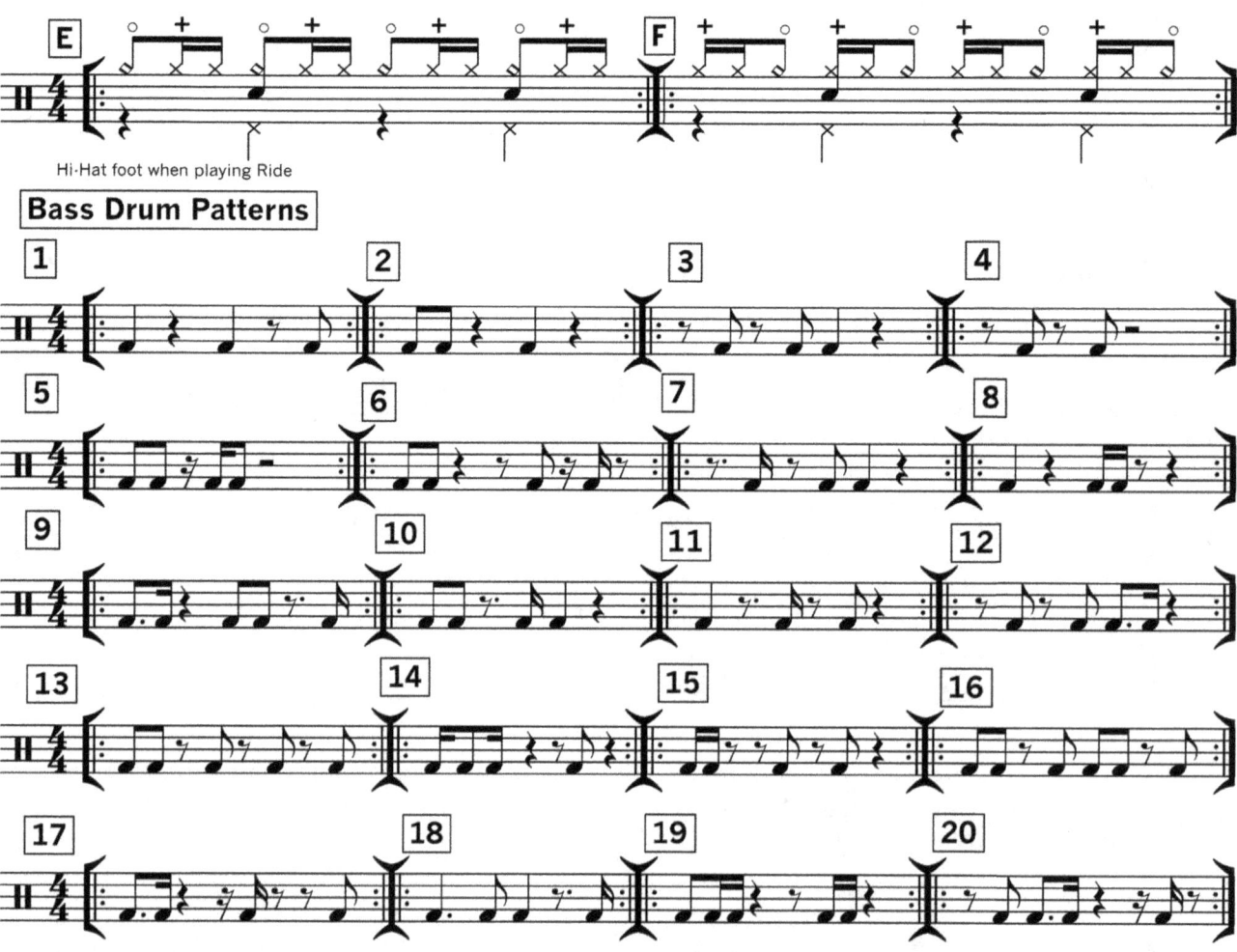

Play E and F with right hand and left hand on the Hi-Hat. Try alternating and bring the hand off the Hi-Hat to the Snare Drum. Also move your right hand to the Ride Cymbal and play the open notes on the bell.

62 Drum Set   Scott Strunk

Triplet Drum Set Coordination

Linear Grooves 1

Linear drumming is a way of playing without layering sounds. Simply by thinking of not layering sounds and playing in a linear way you will develop more ideas and give your drumming a different sound.

♩ = 60-150

Right hand on Hi-Hat or Ride unless marked otherwise.   **Accents on Snare MUST stand out, use 2 stick heights to achieve volume differences.**

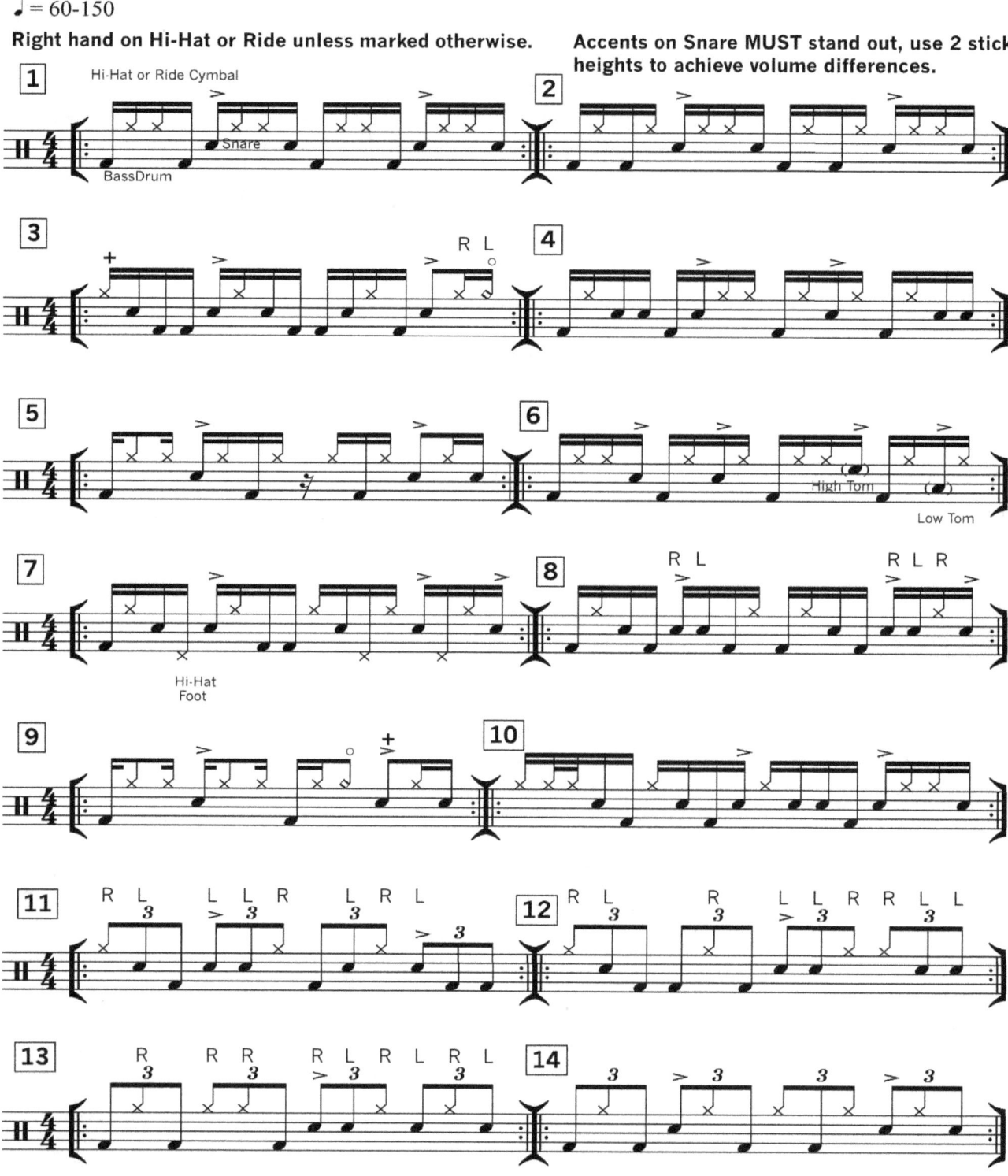

64   Drum Set   Scott Strunk

Linear Grooves 2

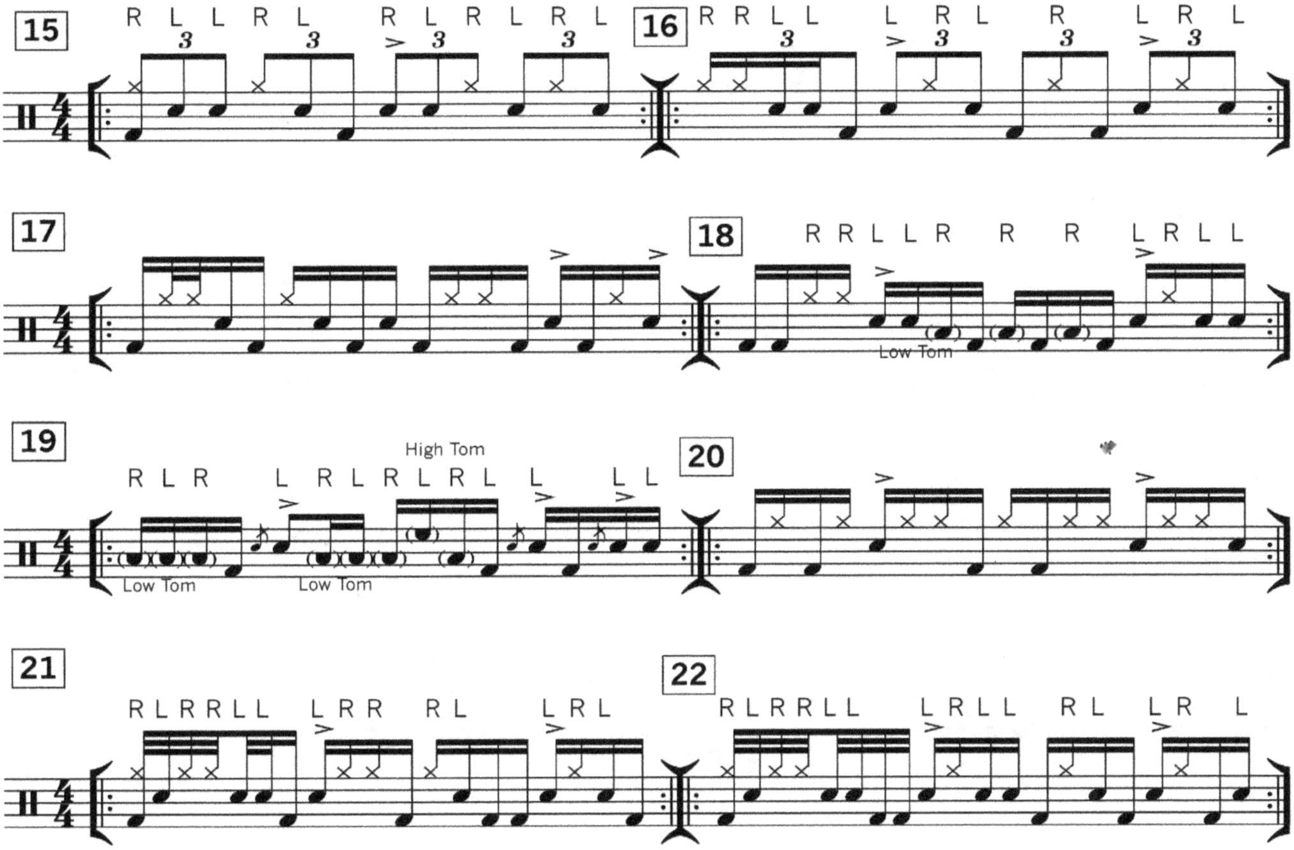

The next 6 bars are saved for you to create your own linear grooves. Have fun!

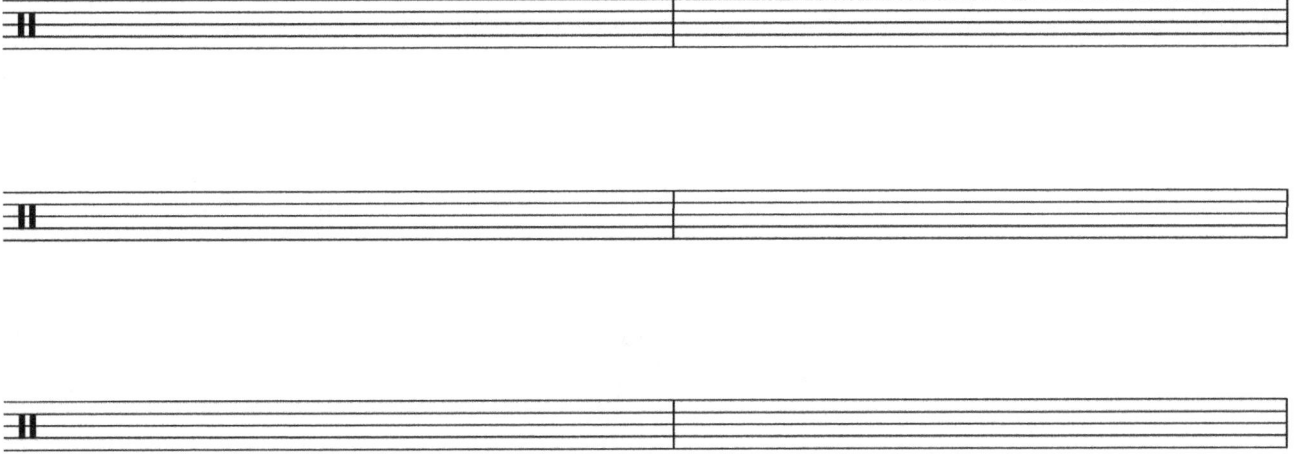

Scott Strunk

Drum Set 65

Fill and Solo Ideas 1

Playing fills and solos can be confusing. Students often ask, "how do I know what to play?" The simplest answer is to choose a fill or solo using the same type of subdivision as the music or beat that you are playing. On the following pages are five subdivisions divided up differently to give you more ideas. Notice that many of the ideas are based on rudiments.

How to practice these exercises: 1. Play as one bar fills while phrasing within a beat. Add a Crash Cymbal on count one of the beat after the fill. 2. Play as a one, two, four, and eight bar phrase that repeats. Add a Crash Cymbal on count one of the beginning of a new phrase. This will signal the new phrase.

66 Drum Set   Scott Strunk

Fill and Solo Ideas 2

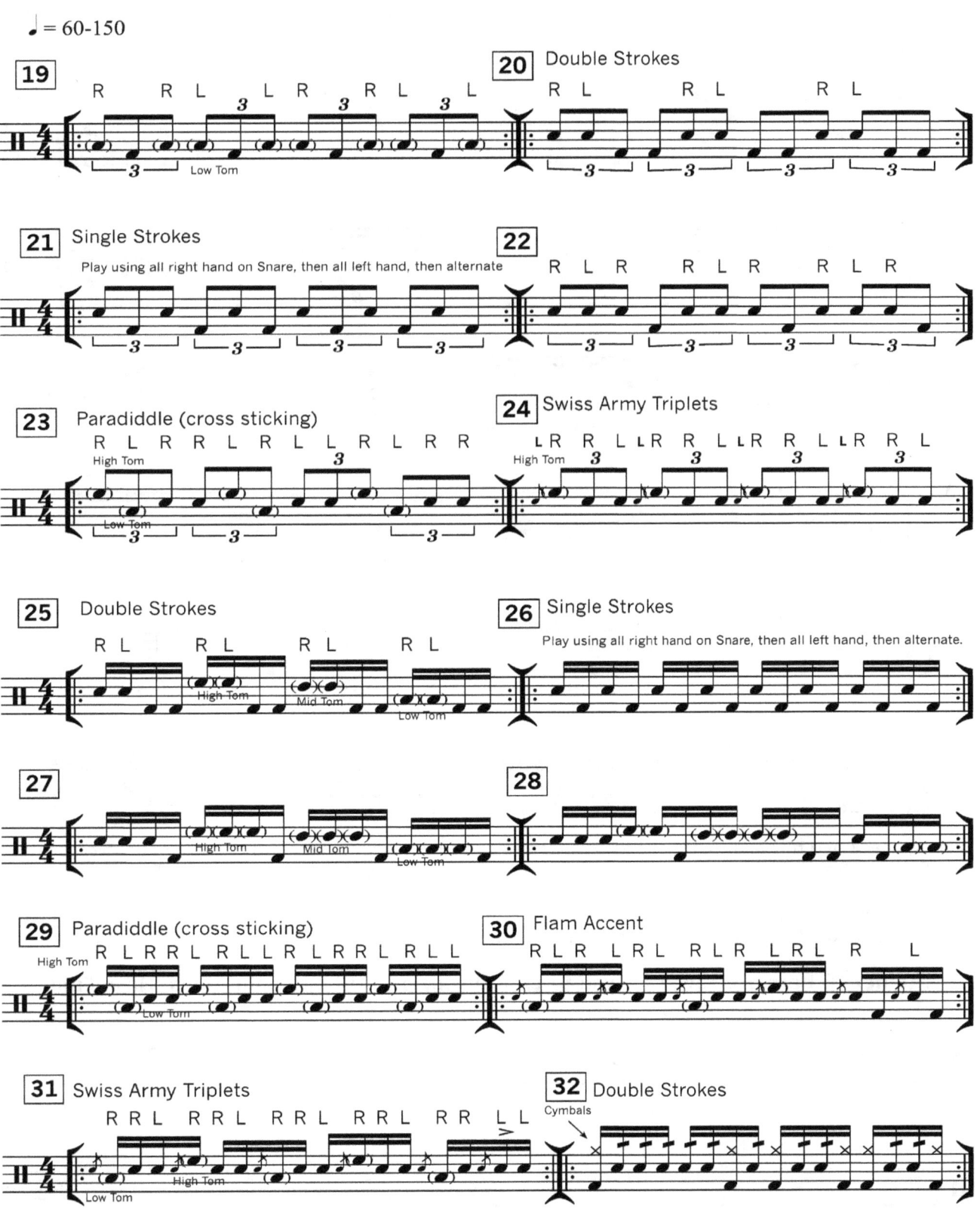

Fill and Solo Ideas 3

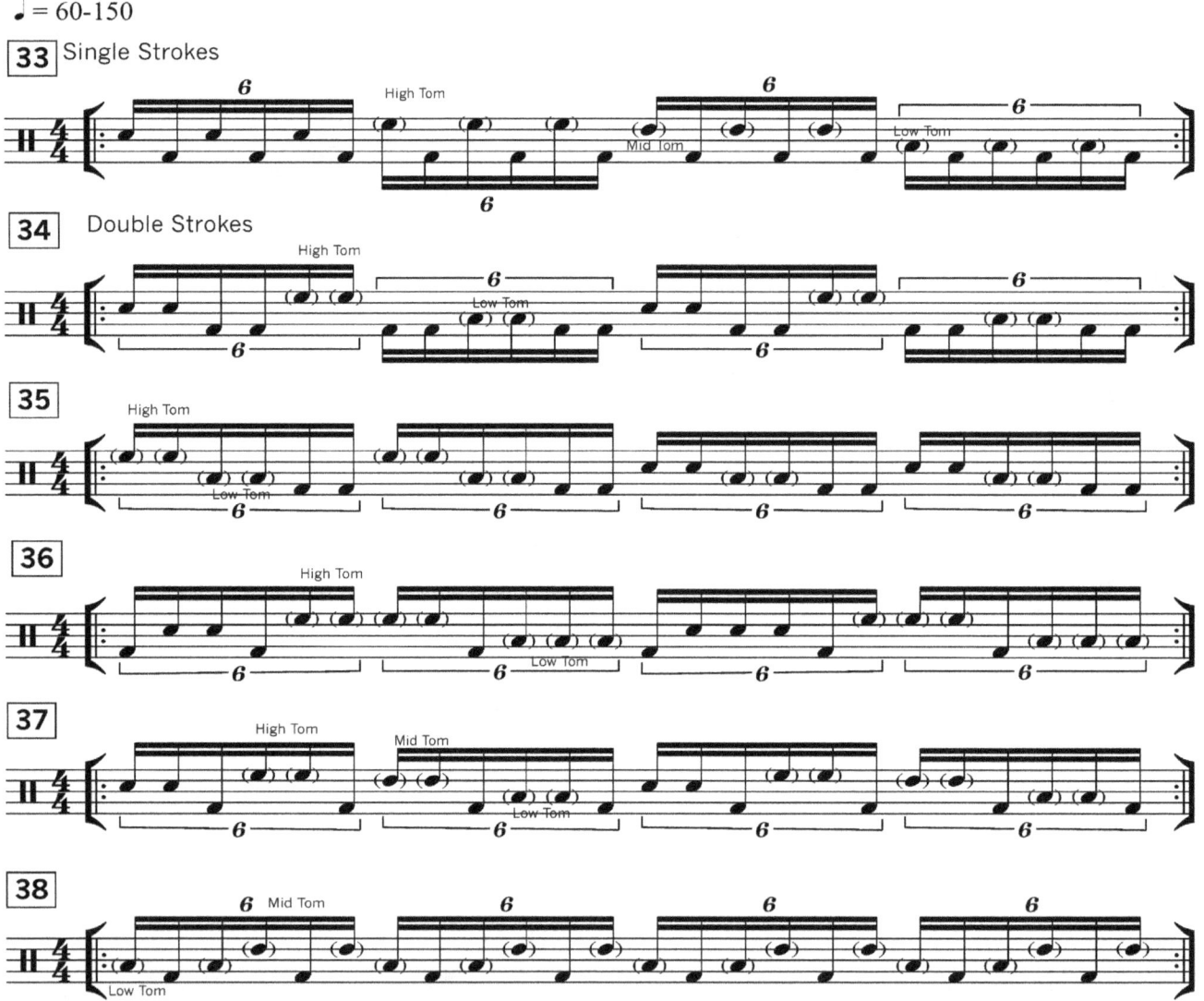

Now go back and mix and match the ideas together as you like. ALSO: Add rudiments, try double stroking the Snare notes at double speed, add other Toms, move Tom notes to Cymbals and Bass Drum.

For another sound add a stick shot to your fills and solos. A stick shot is when you keep one stick on the drum head and hit that stick with the other stick in the middle. You can play a stick shot on any drum.

The next 6 bars are saved for you to create your own fill and solo ideas. Have Fun!

Jazz Time

1. Swinging the 8th notes
8th notes when swung should sound like the first and last note of a triplet.

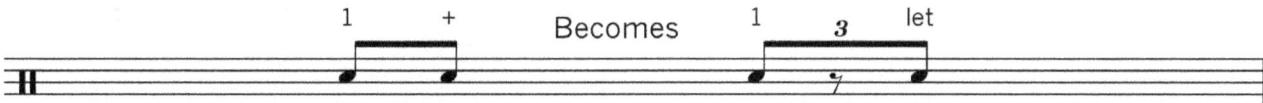

2. Jazz / Swing Time in 4
Jazz time in 4 is when the Bass Drum is on all 4 quarter note counts.

The Ride Cymbal is the most important instrument when playing jazz. Work on getting your Ride pattern to swing by playing with the following motion: counts 2 and 4 should rebound off the Cymbal. Counts 1 and 3 should be played by closing your fingers from the "let" counts and drawing the stick away from the Cymbal with your arm after playing counts 1 and 3. This should all happen naturally while creating a swinging motion and feel. The Bass Drum should be played softly with your heel down. This is called "feathering" the Bass Drum. The Hi-Hat should produce a closed "chick" sound on 2 and 4 with your foot.

Below are 3 ways that you will see jazz time written. In most circumstances each way of writing jazz time will sound like #1. At medium tempos each way should sound like #1. Fast tempos should sound more like #2. Slow tempos should sound more like #3. There is not an exact tempo that you should switch from one subdivision to another. Just be consistent with the subdivision that you choose to play.

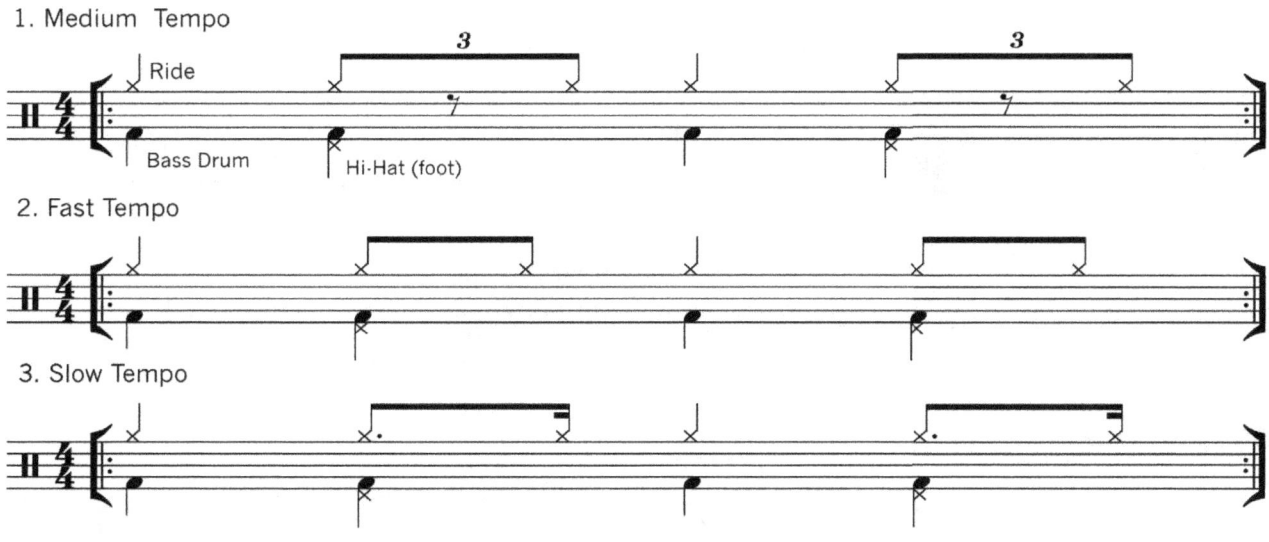

3. Jazz / Swing Time 2 feel
A 2 feel is when the Bass Drum is on 1 and 3.

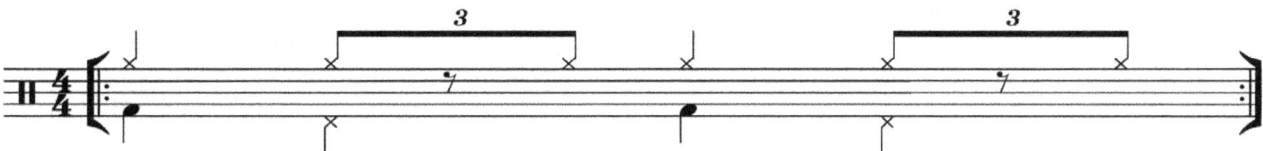

Jazz Time and Coordination 1
Quarter and 8th Note Comping Exercises

♩ = 60-300

Five ways to play this page on Drum Set.

1. Play the following rhythms on the Snare Drum while keeping the jazz time above steady.
2. Play with and without the repeats.
3. Play the following rhythms on the Bass Drum while keeping jazz time in 4 steady on the Ride Cymbal and Hi-Hats.
4. Play the following rhythms on the Hi-Hat while keeping jazz time steady on the Ride and Bass Drum.
5. Play jazz time with a 2 feel while playing the rhythms below on the Snare or Hi-Hat.

Jazz Time and Coordination 2
Quarter, 8th, and Triplet Comping Exercises

♩ = 60-180

Jazz Time — Play jazz time while playing the comp. exercises below.

Also play this page substituting the Hi-Hat foot for the Bass Drum notes above while playing quarter notes on the Bass Drum.

Jazz Time and Coordination 3
Quarter, 8th, and Triplet Comping Exercises continued

Also play this page substituting the Hi-Hat foot for the Bass Drum notes above while playing quarter notes on the Bass Drum.

72 Drum Set   Scott Strunk

32 Bar Tune "AABA" Form

"AABA" form describes the most common form of a song. Many standard songs are 32 bars long and divided up into "AABA" form. Each of the four letters accounts for 8 bars. The first "A" is 8 bars long and then repeats. The repeat is the second "A." The "B" is also 8 bars long and is sometimes called the bridge. The last "A" is just a repeat of the first 8 bars. One time through the whole form is called a chorus. The letters in the following example mark each section of the form.

Play the following rhythms on the Snare and Bass Drum while keeping jazz time steady.

How to play a Cross Stick on the Snare Drum: Turn your stick around and hold your stick at the butt end. Pinch the stick with your thumb and first finger, keep your first finger straight. Lay your hand on the drum and spread out fingers 3, 4, and 5. Lift your stick with your thumb and 1st finger by pivoting on your outside wrist bone. Your outside wrist bone should stay on the drum and the tip of the stick should stick out just below the bottom of your pinky. The stick should hit the rim about 3 inches from the butt end. You can adjust the pitch by sliding the stick and your hand towards the rim or away from the rim.

Play Jazz Standards on the Drums

It is important to think melodically when playing jazz on the drums. Pick some jazz standard tunes from the "Real Book" or other sources. Play the melody of the tunes on the drums while keeping time and soloing. Obviously you can not play the actual melodic notes on the drums, but use the rhythm of the melody and the high to low note shape of the melody to re-create the tune on the drums. For example high note on High Tom, low notes on Low Tom, etc.

In this book I offer many ideas of how to play rhythmic melodies on drums, see the "Playing Time with Melodic Ideas" and "Soloing with Melodic Ideas" on pages 80 and 81 in this book.

Exercise: When you get good at playing the melody, play a chorus of the melody, then a chorus or two of a solo, then repeat a chorus of the melody.

Jazz Beats

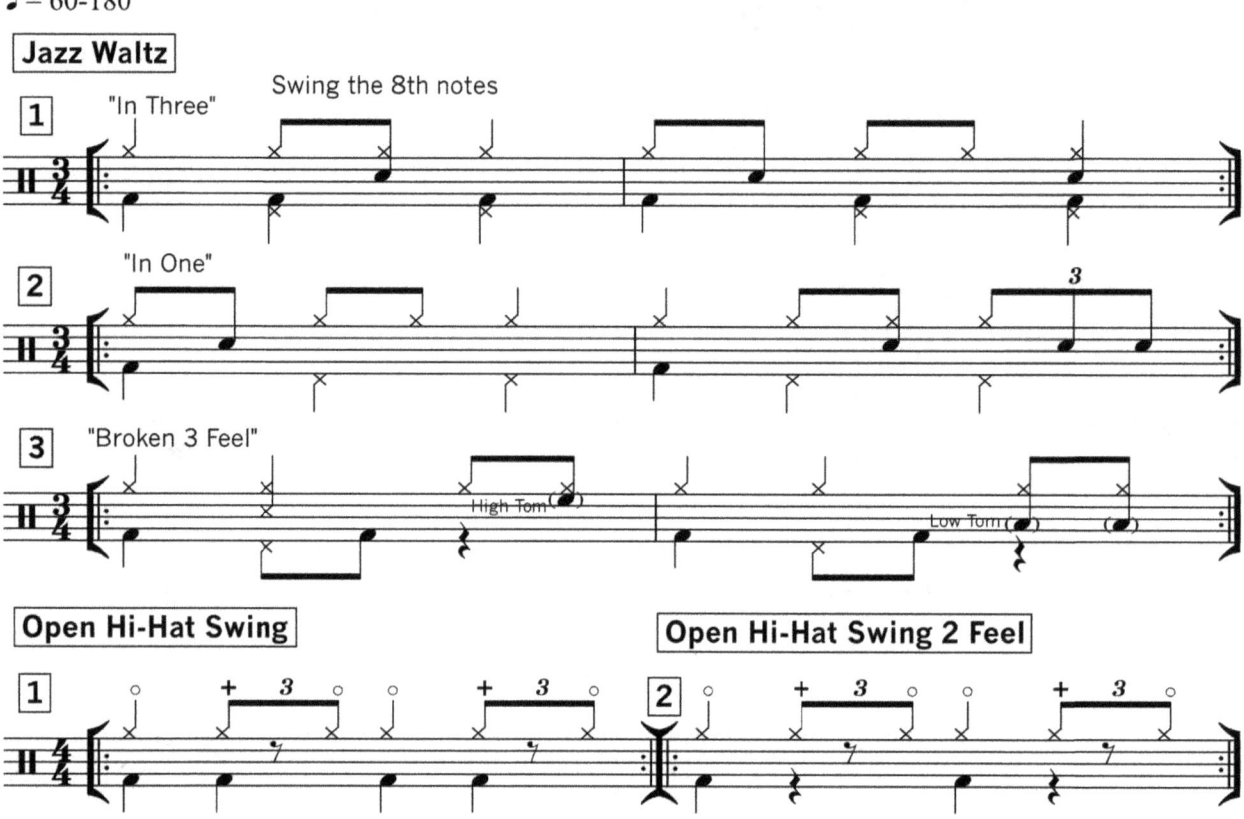

How to play Open Hi-Hat Swing: Keep the Hi-Hat slightly open with your foot at all times. Hold the Hi-Hat with your left hand between your thumb and 1st finger (you can keep the stick in your hand). Let the Hi-Hat have an open sound on 1 the let of 2, 3, and the let of 4. Gently close the Hi-Hat with your hand on 2 and 4. Don't use your foot to close the Hi-Hat.

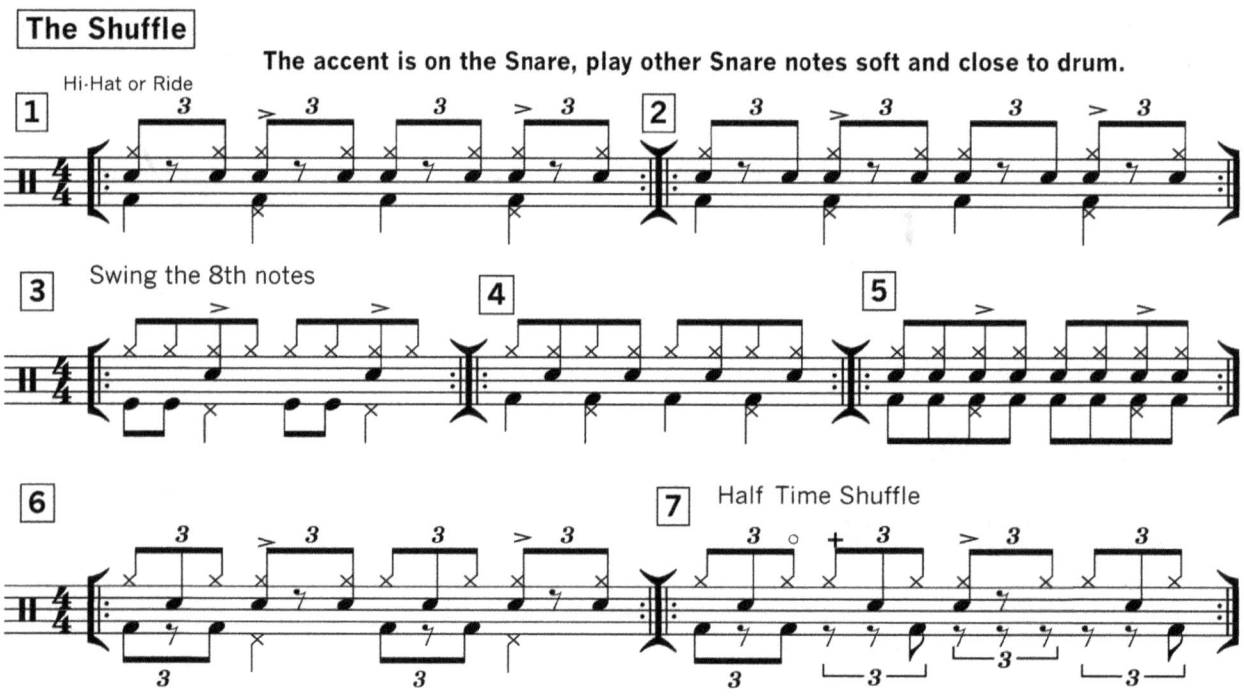

74 Drum Set   Scott Strunk

Jazz Band Audition Page 1

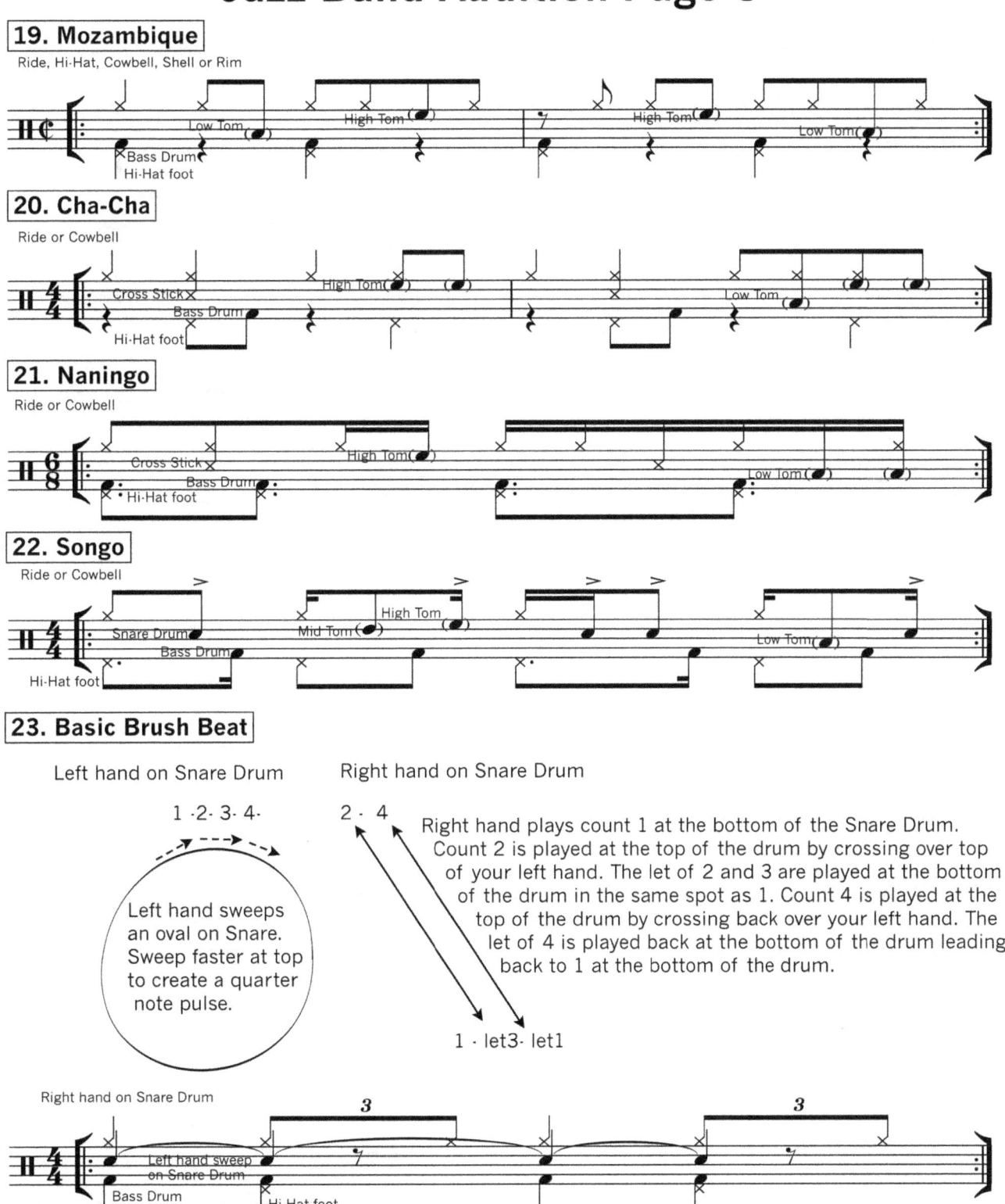

Latin Grooves and Coordination

♩ = 60-180   **Play patterns 1 and 2 while playing the Clave rhythms below.**

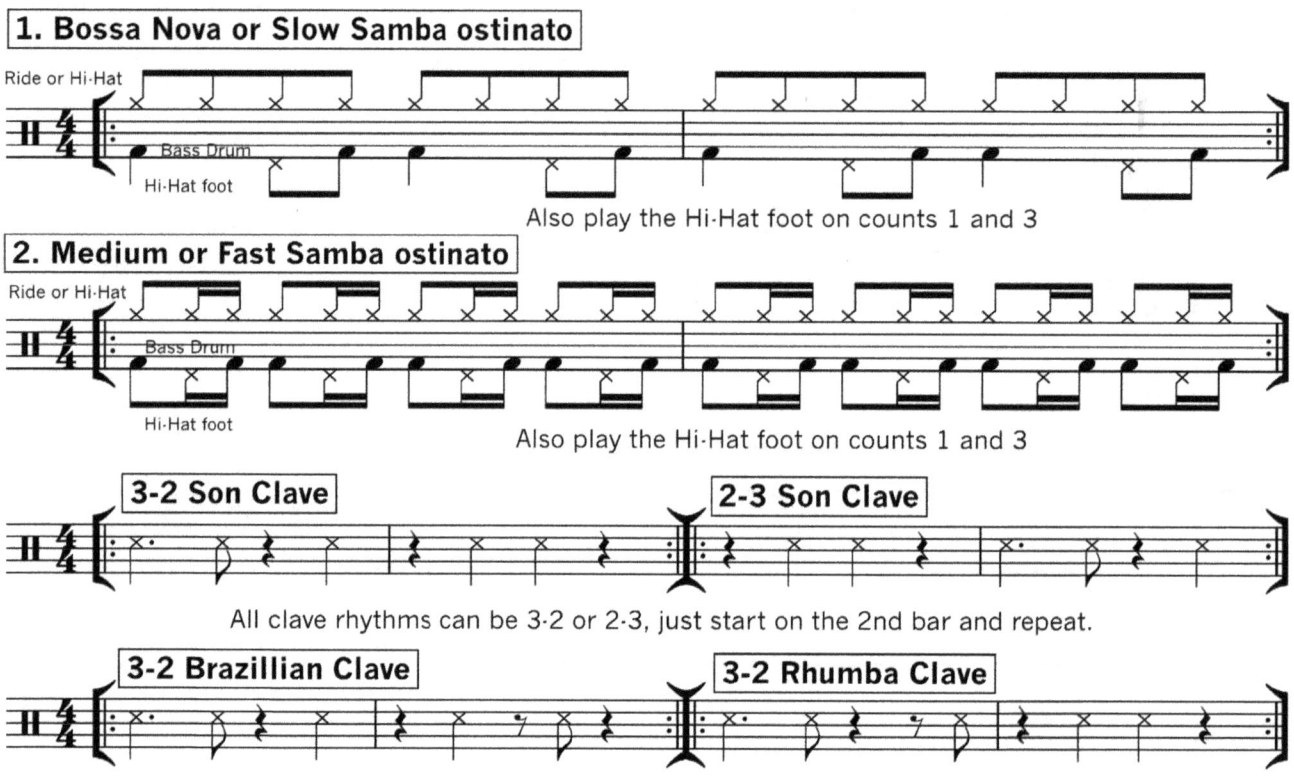

All clave rhythms can be 3-2 or 2-3, just start on the 2nd bar and repeat.

For another challenging exercise, play the syncopation pages in part 2 of this book with your left hand on the snare or cross stick while playing the Bossa Nova and Samba patterns 1 and 2 above.

Cascara Grooves

The word Cascara means "shell." In Cuban music, it is a very important ride pattern. Traditionally the timbale player plays the right hand or ride part on the shell of the drum.

78 Drum Set   Scott Strunk

Grooves in Various Time Signatures

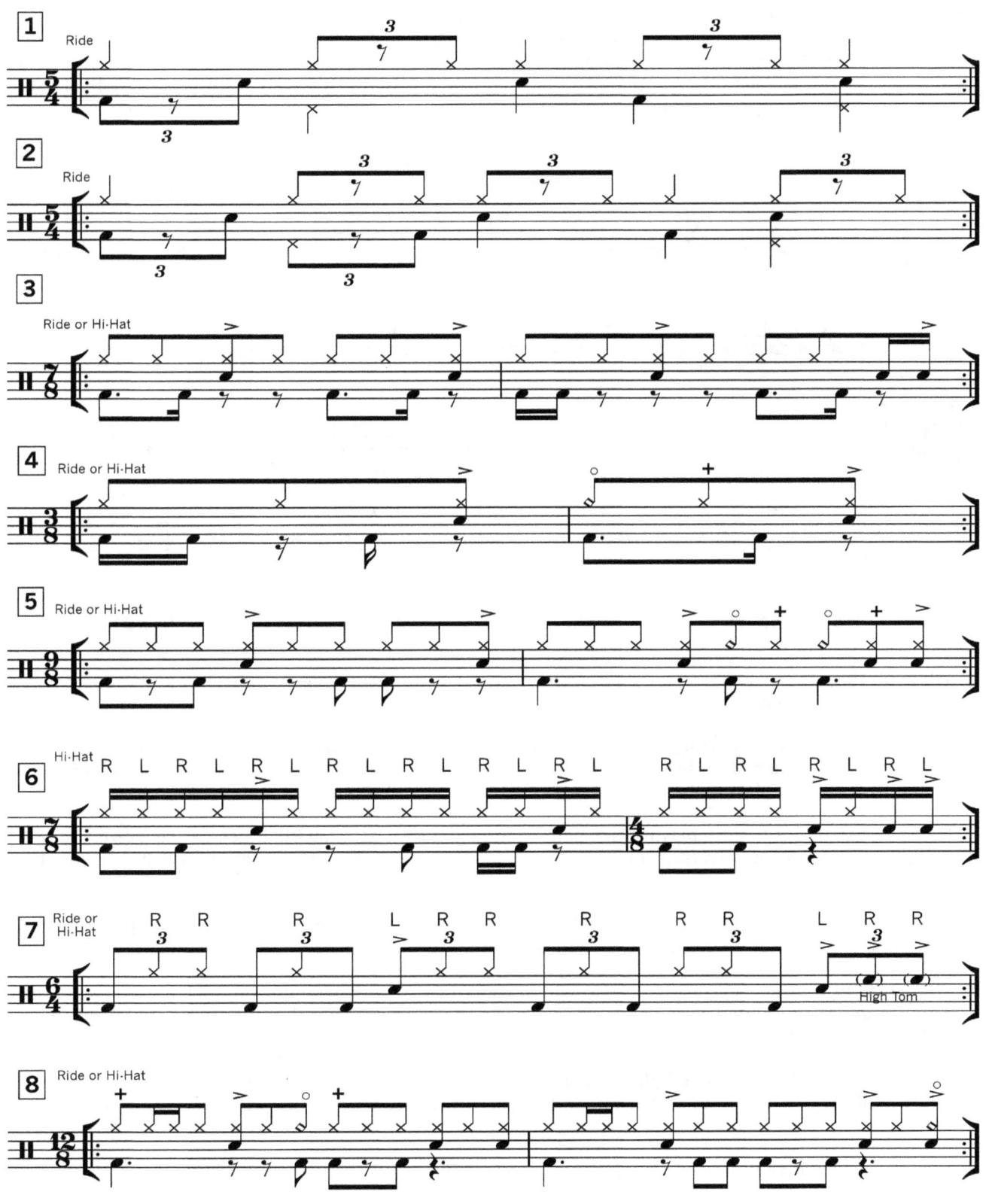

Scott Strunk

Playing Time with Melodic Ideas

When you have a chart put in front of you, you will find rhythms written in or above the staff. Usually, this is not telling you to stop your groove and play the rhythms on one drum. This is telling you to pick up the rhythms somehow on the kit as you keep time going. When you do this, you will be supporting the band and the music by helping to bring these rhythms out of the groove. I have seven different ideas listed below. These are just seven ways of playing time with melodic ideas. When you have mastered these ideas, create your own!

Seven ways to play the rhythmic melody above on Drum Set.

1. While playing jazz time, play the 16 bar exercise on the Snare Drum and Bass Drum while keeping jazz time going and swinging the 8th notes.

2. "Fill in triplets"—while playing jazz time with the Ride and Hi-Hats, add the rythmic melody as instructed in #1 and add fill in triplets on the Snare Drum if you are playing the melody with your Bass Drum. Or if you are playing the melody on the Snare Drum add fill in triplets in the Bass Drum.

3. "Long and short #1"—while playing jazz time on Ride and Hi-Hats, play 8th notes on the Snare Drum and play quarter notes, tied 8ths, or any notes longer than a quarter note on the Bass Drum. Swing the 8th notes.

4. "Long and short #2"—while playing jazz time, play 8th notes on the Snare Drum and play quarter notes, tied 8ths, or any notes longer than a quarter note on the Snare as buzzes. Swing the 8th notes.

5. While playing a Bossa Nova pattern with right hand and the Bass Drum, play the 16 bar exercise on the Snare Drum or cross stick. If you play your right hand on the Ride, play the Hi-Hat on 2 and 4 with your left foot. 8th notes are now straight not swung.

6. "Long and short Bossa"—while playing jazz time, play 8th notes on the Snare Drum and play quarter notes, tied 8ths, or any notes longer than a quarter note on the Snare Drum as buzzes. Play straight 8th notes.

7. Play the syncopation exercises on pages 31 and 35 while playing the six ideas above.

80   Drum Set   Scott Strunk

Soloing with Melodic Ideas

Here are some solo ideas based on the rhythmic melody below. You can use the rhythmic melody of any song to help create a solo based on the tune you are playing. In my experience when drummers are asked to solo, the first question is "well, what do I play?" If you are basing your solo on the melody, not only do you have an idea of what to play, but you will be thinking about the music rather than just the drums. I have listed five ideas below. As always, once you have mastered these, create your own.

Five ways to play the rhythmic melody above on Drum Set.

1. **Play the rhythmic pattern above as accents on the Snare Drum while filling in the missing triplets on Snare Drum. Alternate your sticking.**

2. **Play the rhythmic pattern above as accents on the Toms while filling in the missing triplets on the Snare. Alternate your sticking, which will make the right hand accents on the Low Tom and left hand accents on the High Tom, if you start with your right hand.**

3. **Play the rhythmic pattern above as accents on the Cymbals and Bass Drum while filling in the missing triplets on the Snare. Alternate your sticking, which will make the right hand accents on the right Cymbal and left hand accents on the left Cymbal if you start with your right hand.**

4. **Play variations 1-3 as instructed while double stroking the fill-in triplets.**

5. **Play the syncopation exercises on pages 31 and 35 while playing the four ideas above.**

Picking Up Hits 1

Two ways to play the hits below on Drum Set.

1. Play the grooves in this book and pick up the hits in the music below while continuing the groove.
2. Play a solo in a style from this book and pick up the hits below while you continue to solo.

82 Drum Set

Scott Strunk

Picking Up Hits 2

Two ways to play the hits below on Drum Set.

1. Play the grooves in this book and pick up the hits in the music below while continuing the groove.
2. Play a solo in a style from this book and pick up the hits below while you continue to solo.

Scott Strunk

Drum Set 83

Appendix

How to Practice

Set Goals
With everything you practice you should know why you are playing it and your goal. I'm always amazed at how easy it is to just play and go on autopilot. Before you start playing know how the music should sound in tempo, the technique required, the sticking, etc. Then figure out where you are now and practice until you have filled in the space between where you are now and your goal. A good way to fill in that space is to keep practicing until you can play the piece correctly 4 times in a row. Keep going until you reach that goal. Be patient, it will happen!

Awareness and Detachment
Many times when we play and practice music there are one or two areas that give us trouble. We usually become overly aware of these areas. This is a major problem! This makes us lose sight of the big picture. Now of course you may need to break the trouble areas down and work out the problem until you become comfortable playing them many times in a row. Always be aware of how you sound as you are playing, after all, we are making music! Detaching your thoughts from the one problem will help you be aware of all the important things that you should have established as your goals. This usually helps you get through the trouble quicker.

Practice in Phrases
Practice everything in phrases: 4, 8, 12, 16, and 32 bar phrases. Once you understand and can play something, put it in a phrase. Decide the length of the phrase and count the bars as you play. This is a great way to get used to keeping track of a phrase as you play. By doing this you will eventually be able to feel the phrase. Why is playing in phrases so important? Most music is written in phrases. We are here to play drums in music so we must learn not only to practice notes, beats and fills, but also to play them in phrases. Rudiments, sticking, exercises, beats, fills—all these ideas could and should be played in phrases instead of just playing them individually.

Record Yourself
There is no better practice tool than to hear and analyze a recording of yourself. It's very easy to play something and think you sound ok and in reality you do not! The best way is to hear the truth. When you hear a recording of yourself you hear what worked and what didn't, what felt good or didn't. If you hear a problem it's easier to fix it. For example, you wouldn't have a true idea of how you look unless you used a mirror. The playback of the recording is the mirror of your drumming. Almost every time I have recorded a student for the first time they realized they did not sound as good as they had thought. Recording yourself can help the time you spend practicing be more efficient with immediate, honest feedback.

Practice Performing Correctly the First Time
If you find yourself saying, "I played better at home," it may be time to rethink how you practice. Practice with the mindset of playing correctly the first time you play. Practicing over and over again is important, but at some point you need to be aware that you know how to play what you are trying to play. When you know you have it, go on to something else, then come back to what you were working on. Treat it like a performance! Put yourself under the pressure to play the music correctly the first time you try. By practicing under pressure you will feel comfortable in more situations than just at home.

Don't Always Practice on a Pad

After working out music on a pad, you need to play it on a drum as well. No matter how real a pad may feel, the drum will feel different. Most pads bounce much more than a drum. Also, obviously a drum is louder! Beginning students especially should be aware of how hard they are hitting a pad; the volume of a snare is 10 times louder.

Two Questions to Ask Yourself When You Are Playing

These questions will help you be aware of how you are playing.

1. Am I playing what I am supposed to be playing correctly and in tempo?
If you can honestly and confidently answer "yes" then proceed to the next question.

2. How does it sound and feel as I play?
This should expose any inconsistencies or lack of feel or musicality. Remember it is possible to play something correctly and in tempo and it still may not sound good.

Notes for Band Directors on Using This Book

Band directors should use this book as a guide to help your drummers be all you need them to be. Think of it as a reference to teach from, rather than a method. Skip around in this book and find pages that will help you with where your drummers are at this moment. This book does not need to be followed in sequence. It is important for you to be aware of your drummers' needs and send them to the correct pages. If you need more help, find a qualified private teacher.

Set priorities and goals that every drummer should have in any band.

1. Drummers should be able to play basic subdivisions of notes in tempo and together.

2. Drummers should be able to hold their sticks in a "basic way" that enables them to play rhythms in tempo correctly and evenly. In other words, don't worry about fine-tuning their technique when you need your drummers to play well ASAP! When I say "in a basic way" I mean there are a few "positions" that should happen in order to play proficiently:

- Thumbs should be flat at the balance point of the stick.
- All fingers should gently touch the sticks.
- Elbows relaxed and palms face the floor.
- The quickest way to get to this position is the easy reset on page 2 of this book.

3. Drummers should be able to play evenly and at the correct dynamic level. The ability to play strokes evenly comes from playing with the same stick heights and the same velocity for every stroke. The volume of notes and strokes is changed by stick heights, not by hitting harder or softer. Change volume by changing stick heights. Lift the sticks higher for louder notes and keep the sticks closer to the drum for softer notes.

Music Terminology

Below are some of the musical instructions and expressions most commonly seen in music. A great many of these terms are in Italian because some of the most important composers of the Renaissance period were Italian. For more music terms check out a music dictionary.

Dynamic Markings

pp – pianissimo = very soft
p – piano = soft
mp – mezzo piano = medium soft
mf – mezzo forte = medium loud
f – forte = loud
ff – fortissimo = very loud

Musical Expressions

Accelerando – gradually increase tempo
Adagio – slow, leisurely
Allegro – brisk, lively
Andante – moderately slow
D.C. (da capo) – from the beginning
D.C. al coda – from the beginning to the coda
D.S. (del segno) – from the sign
D.S. al fine – from the sign to the word fine
Fermata – a hold on a note or rest beyond its given length
Fine – end
Grandioso – grand, pompous
Grazioso – graceful
Largo – slowly, broad
Legato – smoothly, connected
Maestoso – majestic
Marcato – marked
Moderato – moderate; at a moderate pace
Molto – much; as molto allegro – very fast
Ostinato – repeated over and over
Poco – little; poco a poco – little by little
Prestissimo – very quick
Presto – quick
Quasi – as if, like
Rallentando (rall.) – gradually slackening the pace
Ritardando (rit.) – getting slower
Scherzando – in a playful style
Segue – follows
Staccato – short, crisp
Subito – suddenly
Tempo – time; a tempo, return to the original tempo
Tenuto – held; a note so marked should be given its full time value
Vivace – vivacious, lively

Recommended Books

This book is a starting point for you to learn the skills required to become a proficient drummer. The ideas in this book are based on the many great drum books listed below. I strongly recommend, as you get deeper into drumming, that you study from these books as well.

Books for Reading Rhythms

Modern Reading Text in 4/4 – by Louis Bellson and Gil Brienes
Modern Reading Text in Odd Time – by Louis Bellson and Gil Brienes
Syncopation – by Ted Reed
The All American Drummer – 150 Rudimental Snare Solos – by Charlie Wilcoxon
Portraits in Rhythm – by Anthony Cirone
Recital Duets for Snare Drum – by Garwood Whaley

Books and Videos for Technique

Stick Control – by George Lawrence Stone
Accents and Rebounds – by George Lawrence Stone
Master Studies – by Joe Morello
Secret Weapons for the Modern Drummer – video – by Jojo Mayer
Great Hands for a Lifetime – video – by Tommy Igoe

Books and Videos for Drum Set

Drum Set Essentials and Time Awareness – by Peter Erskine
Groove Essentials – The Play Along 1 & 2 – by Tommy Igoe
Advanced Techniques for the Modern Drummer – by Jim Chapin
The New Breed – by Gary Chester
The Sound of Brushes – by Ed Thigpen
The Art of Playing With Brushes – by Steve Smith and Adam Nussbaum
Double Bass Drumming – by Joe Franco
Future Sounds – by David Garibaldi
The Drummer's Complete Vocabulary as Taught by Alan Dawson – by John Ramsay
Mastering the Tables of Time – by David Stanoch
Patterns & Linear Time Playing – by Gary Chaffee
Afro-Cuban Rhythms for Drum Set – by Frank Malabe and Bob Weiner
Conversations in Clave – by Horacio Hernandez
The Essence of Brazilian Percussion & Drum Set – by Ed Uribe
The Essence of Afro-Cuban Percussion & Drum Set – by Ed Uribe
The Art of Bop Drumming & Beyond Bop Drumming – by John Riley
The Big Picture – video – by Keith Carlock
The History of the U.S. Beat – video – by Steve Smith

Books for Mental Toughness

Effortless Mastery – by Kenny Werner
The War of Art – by Stephen Pressfield
The Inner Game of Tennis – by Timothy Gallwey
Game Set Life – by Ed Tseng

About the Author

Scott loves teaching drums! Since graduating from Berklee College of Music, Scott has brought hundreds of drummers through elementary school and into the high school band with a foundation of great technique and musical knowledge. He has taught an average of 40 students a week for over 20 years, and participated in hundreds of recordings, live music projects and master classes. Scott also specializes in working with adult drummers who are new to the instrument, or who want to tune up their existing skills. Scott's depth of experience as a teacher and performer puts him in a unique class. Scott has a proven track record of preparing students for auditions at all levels and has helped students earn scholarships to music schools and universities. Many students have gone on to become professional drummers, drum teachers, band directors, and members of DCI drum corps. Scott is proud to be on the Vic Firth education team. Scott also accepts lessons on Skype. You can contact Scott through his web site www.scottstrunk.com or email scott@scottstrunk.com.

www.ingramcontent.com/pod-product-compliance
Lightning Source LLC
Chambersburg PA
CBHW080553170426
43195CB00016B/2773